KURUKSHETRA WITHIN

LEADERSHIP & CONFLICT MASTERY THROUGH THE MAHABHARATA

KAUSHIK BANDIWADEKAR

Clever Fox® PUBLISHING

Chennai • Bangalore

CLEVER FOX PUBLISHING
Chennai, India

Published by CLEVER FOX PUBLISHING 2025

ISBN: 978-93-6707-970-6

"You have the right to perform your actions,
but not to the fruits of your actions."

— Bhagavad Gita 2.47
("Karmanye vadhikaraste ma phaleshu kadachana")

"Whenever there is a decline in righteousness
and a rise in unrighteousness, I manifest myself."

— Bhagavad Gita 4.7
("Yada yada hi dharmasya glanir bhavati Bharata...")

"The mind is the friend of the conditioned soul,
and his enemy as well."

— Bhagavad Gita 6.5
("Bandhur ātmātmanas tasya yenātmaivātmanā jitaḥ")

CONTENTS

FOREWORD

By an Aspiring Spiritual-Corporate Leader

"There is a Kurukshetra in every cubicle, and a Krishna waiting in every conscience."

In today's world, we are more connected than ever—yet more conflicted than ever. Not because we lack intelligence, but because we often lack **inner alignment**. The wars we fight are rarely on literal battlefields anymore. They happen silently—across boardroom tables, in crowded inboxes, in relationships strained by ambition, and within minds torn between personal values and professional demands.

That is why a book like *Kurukshetra Within* is not just timely—it is timeless.

Drawing from the vast, multi-layered universe of the **Mahabharata**, this book is a bridge between **ancient wisdom and modern complexity**. It does not preach; it **translates**. It does not escape into mythology; it **invites you to look into your own life through the eyes of archetypes** we've long admired but rarely internalized.

Each chapter in this book brings alive characters we thought we knew—**Krishna**, the strategist of the soul; **Arjuna**, the warrior of inner conflict; **Draupadi**, the voice of righteous defiance; **Bhima**, the loyal protector; **Abhimanyu**, the bold yet un-mentored youth. And through their triumphs and trials, we are offered a mirror: not just to see the leader we are, but the leader we can become.

As someone who has worked with leaders across industries and witnessed both the beauty and burnout of modern work cultures, I can say this with certainty: **technical expertise is not enough anymore.** Emotional wisdom, ethical clarity, and spiritual resilience are the new non-negotiables.

This book provides a **living framework for those navigating the pressures of leadership, the fog of decision-making, and the pain of conflict**—whether in startups, family businesses, government systems, or global conglomerates.

But more than anything, *Kurukshetra Within* gives permission to professionals to be both **strategic and soulful**—to combine the courage of Arjuna with the conscience of Krishna.

My hope is that this book becomes more than a read—it becomes a practice.

Let it sit not just on your desk but in your decisions. Let it remind you that even in chaos, clarity is possible. And that your greatest leadership challenge is not outside—it is within.

Because in the end, the real battle is not about winning over others.

It is about **winning over oneself**.

— *Kaushik Bandiwadekar*

Aspiring Spiritual Leader | Corporate Warrior | Business Innovator

PREFACE

My Journey: From Corporate Battlegrounds to Inner Wars

By **B. Kaushik**

For over 16 years, I thrived in the world of business—moving across boardrooms, project sites, vendor negotiations, team reviews, late-night delivery calls, and leadership offsites. My career spanned across the **Telecommunications**, **Passive Network Infrastructure**, and **Retail Automation** sectors. From the outside, it was a fulfilling path—marked by success, structure, growth, and recognition.

But as with many professionals in high-performance environments, there came a moment—a pause between two hectic meetings—when I asked myself a silent question:

"If I'm winning on the outside, why do I feel unsettled on the inside?"

That question led me not to a resignation letter, but to reflection. And from there, my real journey began—not through industries, but through **inner landscapes**.

I began studying timeless texts—not as a scholar, but as a seeker. Among them, the **Mahabharata** captivated me not as mythology, but as **a profound leadership manual disguised as an epic**. I saw myself in Arjuna—talented, torn, and questioning. I saw my younger teammates in Abhimanyu—brilliant, bold, and sometimes unprepared. I saw my own silence in Bhima, my frustrations in Draupadi, and, in Krishna, the guide I often wished I had become for others.

As I deepened my spiritual practices, conversations with mentors, and reflections through journaling, I began to see the **parallels between our ancient dharmic conflicts and today's corporate dilemmas**:

- Leadership under pressure
- Navigating ethical grey zones
- Speaking up without burning bridges
- Managing burnout, betrayal, politics, and people
- Finding clarity in chaos
- And most importantly—**responding, not reacting**

This book, *Kurukshetra Within*, was born out of that journey. It is not a memoir. It is a **manual**—for every professional who wakes up each morning to an inbox full of demands and a heart full of questions.

My goal is not to preach or idealize. It is to **equip**. To offer a **practical, grounded framework** rooted in epic wisdom, designed for today's challenges. Whether you are a young executive, a team leader, a founder, or someone simply trying to balance purpose and pay check—this book is for you.

Each chapter brings together stories from the Mahabharata and real-life scenarios from the modern workplace. The idea is not to escape into philosophy, but to bring that philosophy **into your decision-making, leadership, and emotional well-being.**

In my years across industries, I've come to believe this:

It's not technical skill that separates good leaders from great ones. It's inner clarity.

And clarity, as Krishna tells Arjuna, comes from self-inquiry, dharma, and detachment from ego—not from external titles.

So, as you turn these pages, I invite you to not just read—but reflect. Let these insights walk beside you in meetings, negotiations, conflicts, and choices. Let them transform your daily battlefield into a place of growth, not just struggle.

Because in the end, **the real Kurukshetra is not outside you. It is within you.**

And this book, I hope, helps you win not just the war—but yourself.

With purpose and gratitude,

B. Kaushik

WHY THE MAHABHARATA IS THE ULTIMATE GUIDE FOR MODERN LEADERSHIP

When we think of leadership today, we often picture strategy decks, performance KPIs, executive coaching, and fast-paced decisions. But underneath all of that, what truly defines a leader is their ability to navigate **conflict, chaos, and conscience**—precisely the terrain explored in the Mahabharata over 5,000 years ago.

The Mahabharata is not just a story of kings and wars. It is a **realistic, unsentimental, and deeply psychological map of leadership**. It brings to life the dilemmas faced by every professional:

- Should I prioritize loyalty or truth?
- How do I deal with betrayal by someone I trusted?
- When is silence a virtue, and when is it a failure?
- How do I lead when I'm emotionally exhausted?
- What do I do when I'm talented but feel unsupported?

Each character in the epic represents a **leadership archetype** we encounter even today:

- **Krishna**, the wise strategist and conscience keeper
- **Arjuna**, the confused yet capable performer

- **Yudhishthira**, the ethical leader who struggles with practicality
- **Draupadi**, the powerful voice for justice often dismissed
- **Bhima**, the emotionally intense protector
- **Abhimanyu**, the courageous youth thrust into complexity
- **Shakuni**, the quiet manipulator thriving in ambiguity

These aren't just figures of the past—they're **mirrors of our present teams, stakeholders, mentors, and even ourselves**.

What makes the Mahabharata so extraordinary is that it doesn't idealize anyone. Everyone is flawed. Everyone struggles. And yet, everyone is also capable of rising above their limitations through **awareness, dharma, and decisive action**.

As someone who has spent years navigating real-world corporate pressures and organizational politics, I found no Harvard case study or management model that captured the **emotional nuance and moral weight of leadership** the way the Mahabharata does.

It teaches us that:

- Leadership is not about power—it's about responsibility.
- Conflict is not a disruption—it is a mirror of deeper truths.
- Success without self-mastery is hollow.
- And most importantly, every leader must first win their **inner war** before they can lead others into battle.

This book is my humble attempt to decode those lessons for the modern professional—to show that **ancient wisdom isn't outdated—it's underrated**.

Because, whether you sit on a throne or at a desk, the same questions arise.

And the Mahabharata still holds the answers.

– B. Kaushik

HOW TO READ THIS BOOK?

This is not a book to be rushed.

It is a **reflection guide**, a **leadership mirror**, and a **battlefield map**—meant to be read slowly, intentionally, and often, **more than once**.

Unlike traditional leadership books filled with frameworks and jargon, *Kurukshetra Within* is built around **archetypes, emotions, and inner clarity**—inspired by the Mahabharata and grounded in modern professional realities.

Here's how you can get the most out of it:

🌀1. Read with your current role—and inner role—in mind.

Are you leading a team? Navigating office politics? Feeling stuck or undervalued? Struggling with ethical decisions? Use those lived experiences as the backdrop to absorb each chapter. You'll find yourself reflected in more than one character.

📔2. Move through the book in parts—not just pages.

The book is organized into 8 Parts, each centering on a key character or principle:

- **Part I** helps you recognize your personal Kurukshetra.
- **Part II–V** explore timeless leadership styles through Krishna, Arjuna, Abhimanyu, and Bhima.
- **Part VI–VIII** take you through conflict archetypes and actionable strategies.

You can read it sequentially or skip to the part that resonates with your current situation.

✍ 3. Reflect, don't just read.

After each chapter, take a few minutes to pause.

Ask yourself:

- *Where have I seen this pattern in my work or life?*
- *What would a dharmic response look like in my context?*
- *Am I being Arjuna today—or Krishna?*

Use the **reflection prompts, inner practices, and journaling cues** at the end of select chapters to personalize your learning.

⌛4. Return to this book during key transitions.

Leadership isn't linear. You'll encounter conflicts, dilemmas, and decisions many times over. Whether you're:

- Taking on a new role
- Leading a difficult conversation
- Feeling emotionally drained
- Or seeking greater purpose—

This book can serve as your **inner coach**, a quiet but powerful voice of clarity.

---

5. Share and discuss with your teams.

This book isn't only for personal transformation—it's a powerful conversation starter in group settings. Use it in leadership offsites, mentorship sessions, or team retreats. Discuss characters like Bhima or Abhimanyu not just as mythology, but as metaphors for people and dynamics in your workplace.

Final Thought

You don't need to be an expert in the Mahabharata to understand this book.

But by the time you finish it, you may come to see that **your life has always been part of its story.**

So take your time. Pause when needed. Highlight what stirs you.

And if something within you shifts—**even quietly**—this book has served its dharma.

Let the journey begin.

— B. Kaushik

WHO THIS BOOK IS FOR

Professionals. Leaders. Seekers.

This book was born out of my own journey across industries, roles, inner struggles, and spiritual insight. But it is **not** only for those who've lived that same path.

Kurukshetra Within is for anyone who finds themselves caught between **performance and purpose, ambition and awareness, outer success and inner questioning.** If that sounds like you, then this book is your mirror and companion.

👩‍💼 For Professionals

Whether you're early in your career or a mid-level manager navigating complexity, this book helps you:

- Recognize the **emotional undercurrents** of daily work
- Handle **burnout, pressure, and politics** with greater wisdom
- Make career decisions with **clarity, not confusion**
- Stop reacting—and start responding consciously

You'll see your challenges reflected in the journeys of Arjuna, Abhimanyu, Draupadi, and others.

🧑💼 For Leaders and Managers

If you're leading teams, projects, or organizations, this book offers:

- Archetypes of leadership styles that inspire reflection
- Guidance on **conflict resolution, emotional intelligence**, and ethical decision-making
- Real-life stories blended with **epic strategy** to sharpen your leadership instinct
- Tools to lead with both **strength and sensitivity**

Like Krishna, your real power lies not in control—but in **conscious influence**.

🧘 For Seekers

If you've ever asked deeper questions like:

- *What is my dharma?*
- *How do I stay grounded in chaos?*
- *Is it possible to lead without losing myself?*

This book offers you timeless **spiritual answers translated into modern context**.

It helps you understand not just what to do, but **how to be**.

🤝 For Coaches, HR Leaders, and Mentors

Use this book as a **tool for transformation** in leadership coaching, team conversations, and workshops. It offers:

- Universal metaphors to discuss complex topics safely
- Language for emotional truth in organizational settings
- A spiritual-yet-practical lens for difficult conversations

💬 **In essence...**

Whether you're an **executive handling pressure**, a **young professional seeking clarity**, a **team leader managing conflict**, or a **seeker looking inward**, this book will speak to your reality.

Because the battlefield may change…

But the questions of the warrior—and the wisdom of Krishna—remain eternal.

– B. Kaushik

Part I: The Inner Kurukshetra – Awakening the Conscious Leader

1. **Your Personal Kurukshetra**
    - Stress, politics, ambition – the daily battlefield
    - Inner clarity vs. external chaos
2. **The Mahabharata as a Mirror**
    - Understanding archetypes in your workplace
    - How ancient characters reflect modern challenges
3. **Conflict ≠ Destruction**
    - The art of righteous resistance
    - Standing up without burning out

Part II: Krishna – The Master Strategist and Conscious Catalyst

4. **Krishna – Leading Without Authority**
    - Influence vs. Power
    - The spiritual guide as a modern coach
5. **Detachment and Dharma in Decision-Making**
    - How Krishna handles grey zones
    - Emotional detachment for ethical leadership
6. **Timing is Everything**
    - Krishna's mastery of pause, delay, and right action
    - Workplace diplomacy and high-stakes choices

Part III: Arjuna – The Corporate Warrior in Crisis

7. **Arjuna – The Mind of the Performer, the Heart of a Seeker**
    - Talent with self-doubt
    - When high performers freeze
8. **The Bhagavad Gita Moment**
    - Identity crisis and burnout
    - Rediscovering purpose amidst chaos
9. **Decision Fatigue and Emotional Overload**
    - Lessons in resilience and rediscovering clarity
    - Balancing personal and professional dharma

Part IV: Abhimanyu – The Daring Millennial Leader

10. Abhimanyu – Courage in the Unknown

- Walking into complex problems head-on
- Gen Z/Millennials: High potential, high risk

11. The Half-Knowledge Trap

- Burnout in young professionals
- Mentorship and system design to prevent premature loss

12. The Legacy of Sacrifice and Bravery

- Finding meaning in setbacks
- Nurturing new leaders without repeating old mistakes

Part V: Bhima – The Force of Action and Emotional Intelligence

13. Bhima – Strength with Loyalty

- Protecting your team, even when undervalued
- Channelling anger into action

14. When Emotion Becomes Power

- Emotional intelligence vs. impulsiveness
- Bhima's protective instinct as people leadership

15. The Weight of Silence and the Power of Expression

- Balancing internal struggle with external courage

Part VI: Archetypes of Conflict – Lessons from the Fallen

16. **Yudhishthira – The Ethical CEO**
    - Governance, reputation, and long-term thinking
    - Dharma as a compass in business decisions

17. **Karna – The Loyal but Lost Talent**
    - When merit is overshadowed by insecurity
    - Handling resentment and professional rejection

18. **Duryodhana – The Egotist in Power**
    - Leadership driven by entitlement
    - Toxicity and self-sabotage at the top

19. **Shakuni – The Schemer**
    - Office politics and manipulation
    - Countering covert hostility

20. **Draupadi – The Voice of Dignity and Justice**
    - Emotional trauma, resilience, and speaking truth to power

---

Part VII: Strategies to Win Your War – Applied Wisdom for Professionals

21. **Team Pandavas – Building Purpose-Led Teams**
    - Trust, diversity, ego management
    - Collaboration under pressure

22. **Conflict Management the Epic Way**
    - Root-cause clarity
    - Diplomacy, confrontation, and timing

23. The Art of Withdrawal – Lessons from Exile
- Why stepping back can be powerful
- Reflection, reset, and inner mastery

24. The Role of the Conscience Keeper – Being the Krishna in the Room
- Guiding without controlling
- Three Pillars of Krishna's Leadership

25. Rebuilding After War – Healing as a Leadership Skill
- Navigating Aftermaths, Apologies, and New Foundations
- From Survival to Renewal

26. Daily Kurukshetra Practices
- 9 inner habits for balance and leadership
- Journaling, intention-setting, and dharmic decision-making

Part VIII: Conclusion - Be Your Own Krishna and Arjuna

27. Kurukshetra Within
- Integrating wisdom for lasting inner peace and outer success
- From reaction to response – the final transformation

Appendices

- **A1:** The Mahabharata Leadership Archetype Quiz
- **A2:** Conflict Scenarios and Responses
- **A3:** Glossary of Epic Terms for Modern Minds
- **A4:** Daily Dharma Framework for Professionals

PART I

THE INNER KURUKSHETRA – AWAKENING THE CONSCIOUS LEADER

CHAPTER 1

YOUR PERSONAL KURUKSHETRA

"The battlefield is not always a place of bloodshed. Sometimes, it's a conference room, an email thread, or the silence between two colleagues."

The Daily Battlefield

Every morning, we dress not just in formals but in unseen armour. We log in to our emails not unlike warriors scanning the enemy camp. We engage in meetings with half our attention on the spoken word, and the other half scanning expressions, tone, and political undertones. Promotions are fought over like kingdoms, loyalty is tested, and every team has its own versions of Pandavas and Kauravas—some ethical and purpose-driven, others driven by ego, manipulation, or insecurity.

This is the **modern Kurukshetra**.

In the Mahabharata, the war at Kurukshetra was not just a conflict of power—it was a **collision of values**. Today's work environments mirror the same: a place where **ambition wrestles with ethics**, where **stress suffocates purpose**, and where **office politics blur the line between strategy and sabotage**.

We all stand like **Arjuna**, confused and torn.

The Enemy Within

The true Kurukshetra is not outside. It is within us.

- When a deserving colleague is sidelined and we stay silent, **Bhishma** speaks through us.
- When we burn with resentment at someone else's rise, we echo **Karna's** pain.
- When we hesitate to voice injustice, fearing professional backlash, **Draupadi**'s humiliation replays in boardrooms.
- When our ego pushes us to prove others wrong, **Duryodhana** smiles within us.
- When we pause before sending a harsh email, reflect, and instead choose grace, **Krishna** is present in us.

The Mahabharata shows us that **the greatest battles are not fought with others, but with ourselves**—between our higher self and our reactive self.

Stress, Politics, and the Burden of Performance

In today's hypercompetitive world, professionals are caught in an unending spiral:

- **Stress** from over-delivery and under-recognition.
- **Politics** from navigating unspoken hierarchies and manipulative peers.
- **Ambition** often laced with fear—of missing out, of being left behind, of becoming irrelevant.

This tension fuels internal chaos. We move from meeting to meeting, but rarely meet ourselves. The war drums are digital now—Slack pings, passive-aggressive emails, veiled criticism during reviews. Unlike Mahabharata, where the enemies were known, today's enemies hide behind formal smiles and rehearsed politeness.

But perhaps the greatest enemy is our **own inability to pause**, to think, to realign.

Inner Clarity vs. External Chaos

In the first chapter of the Bhagavad Gita, Arjuna collapses—not because he's physically weak, but because he's **spiritually unprepared**. He's confused, conflicted, paralyzed.

> *"I see no good in this war, Krishna."*
>
> **– Arjuna, Gita Chapter 1**

Arjuna had **all the skills**—he was the best archer, the most focused warrior, the most disciplined of all. Yet, in the moment that mattered, **his inner clarity failed him**.

In a similar way, many high-performing professionals today **crumble under chaos** not because they lack capability, but because they lack **clarity**.

The difference between burning out and breaking through lies in your **ability to center yourself amidst the chaos**.

So, how do we cultivate this clarity?

We begin by recognizing three truths:

1. **Not all wars are worth fighting**. Choose your battles, as Krishna told Arjuna—fight not for ego but for dharma (purpose).
2. **Inner alignment precedes outer action**. No decision should be made in haste or emotional turbulence.
3. **Reflection is not a luxury; it's survival**. Just as the Gita was not about adding more information but about rediscovering Arjuna's own clarity, professionals need regular inner dialogue.

Your Daily Kurukshetra Practice

At the end of each day, ask yourself:

- What battle did I fight today?
- Was it necessary, or was it ego?
- Did I act from clarity or reaction?
- Where was Krishna in my day? Where was Duryodhana?
- Did I move closer to peace, or deeper into restlessness?

This simple self-reflection is the first step to mastering the **inner Kurukshetra**.

Closing Thought

The Mahabharata is not a story of the past—it is an **eternal map of the human mind**. The boardroom is your battlefield. The colleagues, your allies or adversaries. Your emails, your arrows. And your **conscience—your Krishna**.

Win the battle within, and no external war can shake you.

CHAPTER 2

THE MAHABHARATA AS A MIRROR

"The Mahabharata is not mythology. It is psychology, sociology, and leadership science wrapped in a poetic narrative."

– From the author's journal

Why the Mahabharata Still Matters

The Mahabharata is more than a tale of war; it is a **mirror to human nature**. Each character, each moment, each dilemma is a **reflection of what we experience today**—in our homes, in our offices, and within ourselves.

Unlike Western myths that end with good triumphing over evil, the Mahabharata doesn't hand out such simple binaries. It doesn't ask, *"Who is right?"* but instead whispers, *"What is right, and at what cost?"* And perhaps that's what makes it most relevant in today's **highly complex, ethically grey, fast-paced professional world**.

This chapter explores how the **Mahabharata reflects the modern workplace**, the challenges of leadership, and the invisible emotional undercurrents that impact decision-making, ethics, and relationships.

Characters as Archetypes in Your Workplace

Let's enter a corporate environment through the lens of the Mahabharata. Every office has:

- **The Arjuna** – the high performer plagued by self-doubt at critical moments.
- **The Karna** – talented, loyal to the wrong leader, always fighting for recognition.
- **The Duryodhana** – insecure, politically savvy, eager for power at any cost.
- **The Yudhishthira** – principled yet often paralyzed in execution.
- **The Draupadi** – dignified, wronged, the voice of ethical questioning.
- **The Shakuni** – the manipulative strategist who thrives on chaos.
- **The Bhima** – emotional, strong, loyal, but occasionally impulsive.
- **The Abhimanyu** – young, brilliant, brave—but not fully equipped to navigate complexity.
- **The Krishna** – the rare mentor who doesn't seek power but empowers others.

We don't just work *with* these people. **We become these people at different times**, depending on the situation, our emotions, and our awareness.

This is why the Mahabharata is not a story **outside** you. It's a story **about** you.

The Crisis of Arjuna – The Modern Executive's Breakdown

When Arjuna dropped his bow on the battlefield of Kurukshetra, he wasn't being weak. He was being *honest.* And for the first time, vulnerability was allowed to take space in the most masculine, duty-driven setting.

Replace the battlefield with your office. Think of a moment before a crucial decision—resignation, promotion, rejection, a betrayal, or a political ambush. We have all dropped our metaphorical bows.

Just like Arjuna, **we freeze not because we are incapable—but because we are conflicted**. We carry responsibilities, reputations, relationships—and yet the inner voice often gets drowned in external expectations.

That's when **Krishna becomes essential**—not as a person, but as a **higher voice within** that guides us back to alignment.

The Slippery Slope of Adharma – The Gradual Compromise

No one becomes Duryodhana overnight. He was not born evil. His entitlement was nurtured, his insecurity was left unaddressed, and his ambition was unchecked. Sound familiar?

Today's work cultures often reward quick wins, unchecked ambition, and subtle manipulation. The line between strategic thinking and political gamesmanship begins to blur. And that's when **adharma creeps in—not in grand gestures, but in tiny compromises**:

- Not speaking up in meetings because the truth may offend.
- Undermining a peer under the guise of feedback.
- Prioritizing visibility over value.
- Choosing silence over courage.

The Mahabharata teaches us that **great destruction begins with small ethical lapses**. And the first step to preventing that is to hold the mirror to ourselves before pointing it at others.

Reading the Epic Through a Modern Lens

Let's reinterpret key elements from the Mahabharata with the modern-day professional in mind:

Epic Element	Corporate Parallel
Kurukshetra battlefield	The modern workplace
Dilemma of Dharma	Decision-making under pressure
Krishna's guidance	Mentorship, coaching, inner wisdom
Arjuna's doubt	Self-doubt, burnout, identity crisis
Exile of Pandavas	Career setbacks, forced breaks, professional ostracism

Epic Element	**Corporate Parallel**
Chakravyuha trap	Complex situations with incomplete knowledge
Draupadi's disrobing	Workplace humiliation, gender bias, silent injustice

The Mahabharata doesn't give us *answers*—it trains us to ask the **right questions**. It nudges us to evaluate not just what we do, but **why we do it**, and what consequences it carries for our inner and outer worlds.

What Makes a Leader in the Mahabharata?

Leadership in the Mahabharata is not about charisma or command. It is about **consciousness**. True leaders are those who:

- Balance **strategy with soul** (Krishna)
- Take **responsibility beyond personal gain** (Arjuna)
- Stand for **principle, even at personal cost** (Draupadi)
- Avoid **the trap of blind loyalty** (Karna)
- Know when to speak and when to act (Bhishma's tragedy was his silence)

It shows us that **technical skills may win wars, but wisdom sustains peace**.

Closing Thought

To read the Mahabharata is to observe yourself. Every chapter reveals not just ancient events, but **recurring patterns in human behaviour**—ego, ambition, confusion, courage, grace.

The boardroom, the open office, the corner cabin, the WhatsApp group—they are all arenas where dharma is tested daily. And in every moment, you are called to choose—**clarity or confusion, wisdom or impulse, Krishna or chaos**.

And that's what makes the Mahabharata not a story to study—but a **mirror to hold up**.

CHAPTER 3

CONFLICT ≠ DESTRUCTION

"War is not the enemy. The unwillingness to face it wisely is."

– Reflections from the Kurukshetra Within

Understanding Conflict: A Shift in Perspective

In most professional spaces, the word **"conflict"** is often used with discomfort. It's considered a threat—a sign of breakdown, instability, or ego. We've been conditioned to believe that **conflict must be avoided** for the sake of harmony.

But the **Mahabharata tells a different story**.

It doesn't romanticize war, but it shows us that **not all conflicts are destructive**, and **not all silence is peace**. Sometimes, avoiding conflict leads to **greater damage** than confronting it head-on. This is one of the most profound leadership lessons of the epic.

Today, in the modern workplace, the failure to understand this truth results in:

- Suppressed voices in meetings
- Unresolved tensions within teams
- Toxic culture disguised as professionalism
- Burnout from emotional repression

When Silence Becomes Complicity

Consider **Bhishma**—the grand patriarch. Wise, respected, capable. And yet, his silence during Draupadi's humiliation remains one of the most criticized moments of the Mahabharata.

He didn't initiate the wrongdoing. But he also **didn't stop it.**

In corporate life, many Bhishmas sit in high positions—good people, technically brilliant, but paralyzed by hierarchy, misplaced loyalty, or fear of rocking the boat.

They watch **ethical lapses**, **abusive power**, **credit theft**, or **gender bias**—but stay silent, thinking it's not their battle.

And this silence eventually enables destruction.

The Mahabharata warns us: **Avoiding conflict doesn't keep the peace. It postpones the war—until it explodes uncontrollably.**

The Role of Dharma in Conflict

Conflict becomes destructive when it is fuelled by **ego, revenge, or insecurity**. But when it is driven by **dharma**—purpose, justice, inner alignment—it transforms into a **catalyst for growth**.

In the epic, Krishna never encourages Arjuna to fight for domination. He asks him to fight for **restoration** of balance, fairness, and righteousness.

Similarly, as professionals, our conflicts must stem not from "I want to win," but from "This isn't aligned with our shared values."

Ask yourself before entering a conflict:

- Am I defending my **ego** or my **ethics**?
- Is this about being **right**, or about doing what's **right**?
- Will this lead to **growth** or simply **venting**?

That shift is the difference between **reaction and response**, between **destruction and resolution**.

Productive Conflict in Teams

True innovation, creative breakthroughs, and healthy cultures arise from **well-managed conflict**. Great teams don't avoid disagreement—they embrace it **with maturity, mutual respect, and shared vision**.

Let's explore three models of workplace conflict through a Mahabharata lens:

Scenario	Epic Reference	Modern Lesson
Suppressed disagreement within a team	Bhishma's silence during injustice	Avoiding tension for too long makes resolution impossible

Scenario	Epic Reference	Modern Lesson
Ego clash between two capable leaders	Arjuna vs. Karna	Talent needs humility; otherwise, it turns into rivalry
Speaking truth to power	Draupadi's court confrontation	Courageous communication drives real transformation

---

Leaders as Conflict Navigators

A true leader does not **prevent** conflict. A true leader **guides it**.

Take Krishna as a model. He doesn't micromanage the Pandavas choices. He listens, advises, and only **intervenes when absolutely necessary**—and when the stakes require higher wisdom.

Leaders today can reflect on these questions:

- Do I allow space for honest disagreement in my team?
- Do I resolve tension or avoid it?
- Do I react to conflict emotionally or lead it constructively?

Transforming Conflict into Growth

To shift your relationship with conflict, use the **5D Framework**, inspired by Krishna's leadership style:

1. **Detect** – Be aware of growing tension. Don't wait until it erupts.
2. **Discern** – Separate fact from emotion. What's the real issue?

3. **Detach** – Remove ego. Respond from purpose, not provocation.
4. **Dialogue** – Encourage open, courageous communication.
5. **Decide** – Take conscious action aligned with dharma, not drama.

Closing Thought

The Mahabharata doesn't teach us to avoid war. It teaches us to **choose our battles with clarity**.

In your professional life, not every conflict needs confrontation. But every conflict needs **awareness**. The more conscious you become, the more you will recognize that **conflict, when handled with grace, becomes a crucible for leadership**.

And so, don't fear conflict.

Fear losing yourself in it.

PART II

KRISHNA – THE MASTER STRATEGIST AND CONSCIOUS CATALYST

CHAPTER 4

KRISHNA – LEADING WITHOUT AUTHORITY

"I am not here to fight your war. I am here to awaken your wisdom."

– Krishna to Arjuna, reimagined

The Silent Leader in the Shadows

He did not wield a weapon.

He did not seek the throne.

He did not own a kingdom.

Yet, **he changed the course of history.**

In a world obsessed with command and control, Krishna's leadership style is quietly revolutionary. **He leads without authority, influences without imposing, and empowers without possessing.**

In today's workplace, where most leaders equate influence with title, visibility, or control, Krishna offers a **radical alternative: strategic detachment and conscious guidance**.

He is not a manager of people. He is a **mentor of minds.**

Leadership without Ego, Strategy without Noise

At Kurukshetra, Krishna drives Arjuna's chariot—not out of subservience, but out of supreme confidence. He knows that **true power lies in impact, not in position**.

As professionals, we often confuse visibility with influence, presence with control. Krishna flips that completely.

His leadership is rooted in:

- **Silence over shouting**
- **Questions over commands**
- **Clarity over chaos**
- **Service over superiority**

Imagine applying this to your role—whether you're a manager, team leader, or individual contributor. What if you led not by asserting control, but by **elevating clarity** in others?

That's Krishna's style.

Detached Involvement – The Ultimate Leadership Paradox

Perhaps the most misunderstood principle Krishna embodied was **detached involvement**—being fully committed to the action, but not attached to the outcome.

In the Bhagavad Gita, Krishna says:

> *"You have the right to action, not to the fruits thereof."*
>
> **– Bhagavad Gita 2.47**

In the workplace, this translates to:

- **Focus on effort, not entitlement**
- **Give your best, release the rest**
- **Don't let success inflate your ego or failure shrink your identity**

Krishna teaches Arjuna not to withdraw from action, but to **transcend anxiety** about its result.

This is immensely relevant to today's professionals who are **burned out not by action, but by expectation**.

Timing is the Hidden Weapon

Krishna's genius lies not just in what he says, but **when he says it.**

He does not give Arjuna the Gita before the war. He waits until Arjuna collapses in moral confusion. In that vulnerable moment, Krishna plants seeds of clarity.

This is the power of **right timing in leadership**:

- A word said too early is ignored.
- A word said too late is damage control.
- A word said at the right moment becomes **transformation.**

Krishna's strategic silence, his delayed counsel, his non-reactive pauses—these are leadership lessons in emotional intelligence, patience, and deep listening.

In high-stakes meetings, crisis situations, or team conflicts—**pause like Krishna**. Speak from presence, not pressure.

The Art of Counsel: Coaching, Not Controlling

Krishna never tells Arjuna, *"Do as I say."*

He asks, *"What will you do, Arjuna?"*

This is masterful coaching.

He does three things that every modern leader should practice:

1. **He listens deeply.** Before the Gita begins, Krishna allows Arjuna to **vent fully**—his fears, confusion, grief.
2. **He reframes perspective.** He doesn't dismiss Arjuna's feelings. He redirects them toward a **higher understanding**.
3. **He hands back agency.** In the end, Krishna says:

"I have told you what I know. Now, do as you wish."

That is **empowerment**, not dependency.

Most modern leaders unconsciously make their teams **rely on them**. Krishna does the opposite—he helps Arjuna **rely on himself**.

Krishna in the Modern Workplace

What would Krishna look like today?

- A leader who doesn't interrupt but **draws out reflection**
- A manager who doesn't micromanage but **trusts deeply**
- A mentor who doesn't impose solutions but **asks catalytic questions**
- A teammate who plays the "charioteer" role—steering without stealing the spotlight

In truth, every team needs a Krishna—**a conscious catalyst**, someone who makes others more aware, more grounded, more powerful.

Becoming the Krishna of Your Own Story

You don't have to be someone's guru or manager to embody Krishna. You just need to be:

- Calm in chaos
- Anchored in clarity
- Present without pride
- Wise enough to lead with humility

In every professional challenge—be it a project dispute, a team breakdown, or a career dilemma—ask yourself:

- **What would Krishna do here?**
- Would he **escalate**, or would he **elevate**?
- Would he **speak**, or would he **pause**?
- Would he **react**, or would he **respond**?

And above all, would he control the moment—or awaken consciousness within it?

Closing Thought

Krishna doesn't fight the war.

He doesn't lift a weapon.

He doesn't take credit.

Yet **he transforms the warrior**.

That is the highest form of leadership:

Invisible. Impactful. Immense.

You may not always be the hero of your organization, but if you choose to be **its Krishna**, you will never be irrelevant.

CHAPTER 5

DETACHMENT AND DHARMA IN DECISION-MAKING

"Act with full presence, but let go of the obsession with outcome. That's the essence of wise leadership."

– Inspired by Krishna's counsel to Arjuna

The Leadership Dilemma: Decision vs. Dharma

In the corridors of leadership, decision-making is celebrated as a skill. From hiring to firing, from investment to innovation, leaders are expected to **make sharp calls, quickly and confidently**.

But what if the decision isn't between right and wrong, but between **right and right?**

Between loyalty and justice?

Between short-term wins and long-term purpose?

This is where most professionals falter—not in lack of knowledge, but in lack of **inner clarity**.

And this is where Krishna's teaching in the Bhagavad Gita becomes eternally relevant.

> *"Perform your duty, established in yoga, abandoning attachment, and become Equanimeous to success and failure. Such equanimity is yoga."*
>
> **– Bhagavad Gita 2.48**

This is not philosophy. It's a **practical operating system for leaders.**

What Is Detachment in the Workplace?

Detachment is not inaction. It's not apathy.

It is **acting with full effort, minus the obsession with reward or recognition.**

In modern terms, detachment means:

- **Making bold decisions without being paralyzed by fear of outcome**
- **Accepting failure without ego bruises**
- **Choosing truth over temporary approval**
- **Letting go of control without letting go of responsibility**

Think of a team leader managing a high-risk project. If they are too attached to impressing the board, they might overpromise, under-deliver, or hide mistakes. But if they stay grounded in **dharma—what's right for the team, the client, and the integrity**

of the process—they'll act wisely and ethically, regardless of how it's perceived.

The Arjuna Moment – Doubt Before Action

Arjuna had fought hundreds of battles before Kurukshetra. What stopped him here was not the opponent—but the **emotional weight of the decision**.

He was torn between two dharmas:

- His **Kshatriya duty** (to fight injustice)
- His **familial loyalty** (to elders and cousins)

Leaders today face similar crossroads:

- Do I speak up against my senior's decision, or protect my position?
- Do I promote the most qualified candidate, or the politically safe one?
- Do I scale at the cost of culture, or grow slower with integrity?

When we try to please everyone or avoid inner discomfort, **we postpone the right decision**.

Krishna tells Arjuna:

> *"You grieve for those who should not be grieved for, yet you speak words of wisdom. The wise do not mourn the living or the dead."*
>
> **– Bhagavad Gita 2.11**

In essence: **Don't wrap emotional confusion in the language of reason. Choose dharma with clarity, not compromise.**

Clarity Precedes Decision

Before Arjuna lifts his bow again, Krishna gives him only one gift—**clarity**.

This is a profound leadership insight: **The best decisions are made not in stress, but in stillness.**

Here's a modern decision-making model inspired by Krishna's wisdom:

◈ The 4C Framework for Dharmic Decision-Making

1. **Context**
   - What's the reality? What's at stake—people, principles, priorities?
2. **Clarity**
   - Strip ego and fear. What aligns with your core values and purpose?
3. **Courage**
   - Are you willing to choose the harder right over the easier wrong?
4. **Consequences**
   - Can you accept the outcome without regret or bitterness?

This model doesn't guarantee success. But it guarantees that you **remain in alignment with your higher self**, which is the only compass that never fails.

The Myth of Control

Modern professionals are burdened with the illusion that they must **control everything**—outcomes, perceptions, timelines, even people.

But Krishna dismantles this myth:

> *"Let your concern be with action alone, and never with the fruits of action."*
>
> **– Bhagavad Gita 2.47**

You don't own the outcome. You only own your **intention and action**.

When leaders truly embody this:

- They lead with presence, not pressure
- They give feedback without controlling response
- They innovate without fearing failure
- They trust the process, not just the projection

This is the difference between **ego-driven leadership** and **soul-led leadership**.

Detachment Does Not Mean Indifference

Let's be clear—Krishna is **not promoting passivity**.

He never tells Arjuna to quit the battlefield. He tells him to fight, but from a **place of centered awareness**, not emotional reaction.

Likewise, in your role:

- Don't become numb to outcomes—be **aware**, not **attached**
- Don't escape tough conversations—engage with empathy, not anxiety
- Don't withdraw from risk—act from wisdom, not worry

Detachment enhances action. It makes you sharper, calmer, and far more effective.

Closing Thought

In the Mahabharata, those who act with **attachment**—Duryodhana with his ego, Karna with his loyalty, Bhishma with his vows—end up in **conflict with themselves.**

Krishna stands apart—**fully involved, yet completely free.**

Leadership in today's world demands the same mastery:

- Be fully committed, yet never consumed
- Lead with clarity, not compulsion
- Make decisions not to control the future, but to honour the present

This is the essence of **dharmic leadership**—and the true path to **inner peace and outer excellence.**

CHAPTER 6

TIMING IS EVERYTHING – KRISHNA'S SUBTLE POWER PLAY

"A wise word said too early is noise. The same word said at the right time becomes transformation."

– Inspired by Krishna's silence before the Gita

The Underestimated Weapon: Time

In modern business culture, speed is worshipped. We glorify fast replies, quick decisions, and instant launches. **Urgency is seen as effectiveness.**

But Krishna, the greatest strategist in the Mahabharata, teaches us something radically different:

Right timing > Rapid timing.

He speaks only when the moment demands.

He acts not because he can, but because **it's time**.

He waits—not out of laziness, but **because silence is sometimes the strongest leadership move**.

As professionals, we often feel pressured to **react instantly**—to a conflict, a request, or a crisis. But true wisdom lies in **pausing to sense the right moment**.

The Gita Was Not Delivered in Peace

Let's remember this:

Krishna did **not** teach Arjuna the Bhagavad Gita **in the palace**.

He waited till Arjuna broke down on the battlefield.

That moment of **inner collapse** was **perfectly timed**—not for Arjuna's ego, but for his evolution.

In the modern workplace, imagine this same principle:

- A senior leader notices a high performer spiralling into burnout. Instead of intervening too early, they **wait, observe, allow the breakdown**, and then step in to coach—not to save, but to empower.
- A team member is pushing for recognition. Instead of validating prematurely, the leader **waits until the contribution becomes unmistakable**—and then celebrates it with sincerity and impact.

Timing is not delay. **Timing is respect for readiness.**

Why Leaders Must Master the Pause

We often say the wrong thing at the wrong time:

- Feedback given when someone is emotionally raw = damage.
- Praise delayed until after a resignation = regret.
- A solution offered before a person is ready to hear it = resistance.

Krishna shows us how **the pause is a leadership tool**, not a sign of indecision.

In his many roles:

- He delays entering the war until both sides **reveal their true intentions**.
- He watches Bhishma and Drona fall, knowing that the **cycle of karma must play out**.
- He only speaks the Gita when Arjuna is **receptive**, not reactive.

Apply this at work:

- Pause before replying to a provocative email.
- Pause before correcting someone in public.
- Pause before giving advice—first ask, *"Are they ready for it?"*

"Silence is not absence. It is preparation."

Understanding Kairos – The Right Moment

Ancient Greeks had two words for time:

- **Chronos** – the clock (measurable time)
- **Kairos** – the moment (qualitative time)

Krishna operated in **Kairos**. He wasn't chasing schedules—he was tuning into **alignment**.

As professionals, we spend all day on Chronos—deadlines, meetings, reminders. But what we need more of is **Kairos**—that deep, intuitive sensing of when it's time to act, speak, or decide.

This intuitive timing is **sharpened by silence**, **strengthened by reflection**, and **guided by detachment**.

Strategic Timing in Conflict Resolution

Timing is everything when handling conflict. A well-intentioned action done at the wrong time can:

- Escalate tension
- Deepen misunderstanding
- Damage relationships

Learn from Krishna:

- When Draupadi was humiliated, Krishna did not go to war immediately. He **planted seeds of consequence**.
- When Karna was vulnerable before the war, Krishna tried to elevate him—not shame him.

- When Shakuni schemed, Krishna **did not counter every move with logic**. He let the trap build itself.

Sometimes, **your opponent's momentum becomes their downfall**.

You don't need to stop them—just **step aside, and let time do its work**.

Using Timing in Leadership: A Practical Guide

Here are five areas where Krishna-style timing can be practiced in leadership:

Situation	What Most People Do	What Krishna Would Do
Giving feedback	React immediately	Wait for calm + openness
Making decisions	Rush to avoid uncertainty	Pause for clarity
Handling mistakes	Blame instantly	Understand context first
Coaching others	Preach from the start	Wait for readiness
Delivering hard truths	Avoid or rush	Prepare the ground first

---

Trusting the Unseen Rhythms

Sometimes, leadership is not about what you do—it's about **when you do it**.

This requires deep **emotional intelligence**, **patience**, and **faith in timing**.

There will be times when:

- You want to confront someone, but it's wiser to **wait**.
- You want to launch a new idea, but it's better to **incubate**.
- You want to fix a team dynamic, but it needs **to break first** for real healing to happen.

Krishna never rushed the transformation. He **guided it through time**.

Closing Thought

Timing is not a skill. It's a **spiritual discipline**.
It asks of you to trust your silence more than your speech.
To value readiness more than urgency.
To lead not by pressure, but by presence.
So the next time you face a decision, a conflict, or a conversation—ask not just:

"What should I do?"

Ask instead:

"Is it the right time to do it?"

Because sometimes, the pause **is the leadership**.

PART III

ARJUNA – THE CORPORATE WARRIOR IN CRISIS

CHAPTER 7

ARJUNA – THE MIND OF THE PERFORMER, THE HEART OF A SEEKER

"Arjuna wasn't afraid to fight. He was afraid to fight the people he loved, in a war he didn't ask for."

– Reflection on the modern leader's dilemma

The Crisis of the Capable

Arjuna was everything the world celebrates:

- Skilled
- Disciplined
- Respected
- Trusted
- Spiritually inclined
- Emotionally intelligent

And yet, at the decisive moment, when the conch shells blew and the war of Kurukshetra was to begin, Arjuna's **inner world collapsed**.

"My limbs give way, my mouth is dry, my body trembles. I see omens of misfortune, O Krishna. I will not fight."

– Bhagavad Gita 1.28–30

This was not the breakdown of a weak man.

This was the **awakening of a sensitive soul** in the face of brutal reality.

Arjuna stands today as a timeless symbol of the **high-performing professional on the verge of burnout**—caught between duty and despair, results and relationships, ambition and ethics.

The Hidden Pain of High Performers

In every organization, we meet modern-day Arjuna's. They are:

- The dependable managers who never say no.
- The project leads who hold teams together.
- The rising stars who carry the expectations of many.
- The individuals who **excel outwardly**, but often suffer **silently**.

They struggle not with skill, but with **self-alienation**.

They ask:

- *Am I fighting the right battles?*
- *Is this promotion worth the pressure it brings?*
- *Why does success feel so empty sometimes?*
- *Why do I feel guilty even when I win?*

Like Arjuna, their hands don't tremble in front of the challenge—they tremble in front of **conflicted meaning**.

Why Arjuna's Breakdown Matters

Our culture often shames breakdowns.

We call them weakness, failure, and instability.

But Arjuna's breakdown gave birth to the **Bhagavad Gita**—the world's most enduring scripture on inner clarity and purposeful action.

That means:

- Your breakdown is not the end. It may be the beginning of **deeper wisdom**.
- Your moment of pause is not failure. It may be your **gateway to clarity**.
- Your doubts don't disqualify you from leadership. They **humanize** your leadership.

Krishna didn't dismiss Arjuna's collapse. He stayed with him. He held space. And then he gently **reframed the narrative**.

This is how we must treat our own inner Arjuna—and others' too.

When the Inner Voice Becomes Distant

Arjuna's greatest confusion wasn't about the war. It was about **himself**.

"What use is victory, kingdom, or pleasures if they come at the cost of peace within?"

In modern workplaces, we're taught to align with:

- KPIs
- Goals
- Quarterly numbers
- Stakeholder satisfaction

But no one teaches us to align with our **inner compass**.

Arjuna's dilemma reminds us that:

- Not all performance is **purposeful**
- Not all victories feel like **success**
- Not all duties are **yours to carry**

Sometimes, like Arjuna, we need to **put down the bow**. To pause. To ask deeper questions.

The Strength in Vulnerability

In that moment of vulnerability, Arjuna does something rare:

He asks for help.

"I am your disciple, Krishna. Guide me. I do not know what to do."

Modern leaders often resist this move. Asking for help feels like losing authority. But, Krishna doesn't see it as a weakness. He sees it as the **beginning of transformation**.

In that humility, Arjuna reclaims his greatest power—not his arrows, but his **awareness**.

Your growth as a leader doesn't come from knowing all the answers.

It comes from knowing when you are lost—and choosing to seek clarity.

Reclaiming Purpose Amidst Chaos

Krishna doesn't advise Arjuna to withdraw from the war.

He doesn't sugar-coat it either.

He helps Arjuna see that his **confusion is real**, but it doesn't have to become his **identity**.

Likewise, you may be facing:

- A toxic environment
- Conflicting team dynamics
- Ethical grey zones
- Unreasonable expectations

Instead of quitting or complying, **pause and realign**. Ask:

- What is my dharma here?
- Am I acting out of fear, guilt, or clarity?
- What would a higher version of me choose now?

The battle doesn't need to be avoided. It needs to be **reframed**.

Signs You Are in an Arjuna Moment

Here are subtle signs that you, or someone on your team, may be facing an "Arjuna moment":

- You begin to feel **disconnected from your work**, even though nothing external has changed.
- You carry a **constant low-level guilt** about underperforming, despite delivering well.
- You are **questioning the purpose** of what you're doing, even though you're climbing fast.
- You begin to crave **silence and meaning**, not just success.
- You fear that **if you stop and reflect**, everything may fall apart.

These moments are not breakdowns. They are **calls to inner awakening**.

From Seeker to Warrior – The Integration

After the Gita, Arjuna doesn't stop being a seeker.

He becomes a **grounded seeker**—clear, calm, committed.

That is the goal of every modern professional:

To integrate the warrior and the seeker.

- To act from purpose, not pressure
- To perform with grace, not grinding
- To grow with depth, not just ambition
- To succeed without selling the soul

The Gita isn't about withdrawal. It's about **realignment**.

Closing Thought

Arjuna teaches us that true strength is not in how many targets you hit, but in how **aligned you are while shooting**.

His greatest achievement wasn't winning the war. It was **fighting it with inner clarity**, without rage or ego.

That's the new professional model of leadership—not robotic hustle, but **conscious, purpose-led performance**.

So if you're ever in doubt, disillusioned, or disconnected from your path, remember:

It's not a breakdown.

It's your **Bhagavad Gita moment**.

CHAPTER 8

THE BHAGAVAD GITA MOMENT

"When the performer within you collapses, the seeker awakens. That's your Gita moment."

– From the margins of a high-performing mind

The Collapse Before the Clarity

Before the wisdom of the **Bhagavad Gita** flowed from Krishna's lips, there was **silence**—not external silence, but the stunned, heavy stillness of a warrior who had lost all will to fight.

Arjuna was not afraid of defeat.

He was terrified of **what the victory would cost**.

He was watching his identity unravel in real time:

- The protector
- The noble warrior
- The family man
- The righteous brother

And in that moment of collapse, Krishna didn't say:

"Be strong."

He said:

"Be still. Reflect. See clearly."

Every modern professional has a **Bhagavad Gita moment**.

Not in a battlefield, but in:

- The boardroom, before a hard truth must be spoken.
- The late night, when you wonder why you feel so empty despite success.
- The resignation letter you hesitate to submit.
- The moment you realize you're performing not out of purpose, but under pressure.

Burnout: The Modern Kurukshetra

Burnout isn't just exhaustion.

It is a **crisis of meaning**.

You're working long hours—but don't know why.

You're achieving goals—but they no longer excite you.

You're surrounded by people—but feel misunderstood.

You're wearing the title—but lost the voice within.

This is not laziness. This is not a weakness. This is **Arjuna at Kurukshetra**—someone who can no longer fight a war that doesn't make sense.

Krishna does not drag Arjuna back into battle.

He invites him to **reclaim his own reasons to fight**.

Three Layers of Identity Collapse

When the Gita begins, Arjuna is shattered. His disintegration follows three layers, and each one reflects the modern professional journey:

1. **Role Collapse**

"What is the point of being a warrior, if my sword harms those I love?"

This is when the title you carry (Manager, CEO, Artist, Engineer) no longer carries *you.*

2. **Relational Collapse**

"These are not enemies. They are teachers, cousins, elders."

You begin to see that the structures you built your life upon—family, friendships, professional loyalties—are far more complex than black-and-white roles.

3. **Moral Collapse**

"Is winning still noble if it means destroying peace within?"

This is when external success comes at an internal cost. And suddenly, your compass spins wildly.

Burnout is not caused by too much work.

It is caused by working too long without connection to your **why**.

The Gita as a Manual for Realignment

Krishna's words in the Gita are not about war tactics.

They are about **realignment with your higher identity**.

"You are not the body. You are not the roles you play. You are the eternal self that witnesses it all."

For the modern professional, this is a reset button:

- You are not just a designation.
- You are not the expectations placed on you.
- You are not your LinkedIn summary.

You are the **consciousness navigating through experience**.

This isn't a philosophical escape.

It's **operational freedom**.

Because when you stop clinging to your titles, fears, and anxieties, you begin to **act from calm, not chaos**.

Turning Breakdown into Breakthrough

The Gita doesn't remove the war.

It doesn't remove Arjuna's pain.

It simply **clears the fog**.

Burnout doesn't need you to quit everything.

It needs you to pause long enough to ask:

- *Is this path aligned with who I am now—not who I was five years ago?*
- *Am I acting from clarity or compulsion?*
- *Is my ambition rooted in joy or fear?*

When these questions are answered honestly, **a quiet strength returns**. The bow rises again—not with tension, but with truth.

How to Recognize Your Gita Moment?

You may be in a Bhagavad Gita moment if:

☑ You're functioning at high output, but feel disconnected inside

☑ You're questioning long-held ambitions or goals

☑ You feel emotionally drained by the roles you play

☑ You secretly wonder, "Who am I without this identity?"

☑ You crave solitude—not escape, but insight

The good news is: This is not your end.

This is your **Kurukshetra within**—and like Arjuna, you're ready for **a higher version of your path**.

What to Do in Your Gita Moment

Like Krishna did for Arjuna, here's a framework to realign:

1. **Pause**

Stop acting out of habit. Silence isn't stagnation. It's space for wisdom to enter.

2. **Witness**

Journal your confusion. Speak with someone who won't fix you, but listen deeply.

3. **Reframe**

Not "What am I doing wrong?" but "What no longer aligns with who I am becoming?"

4. **Recommit**

Return to action—but now from your center, not your survival instincts.

5. **Detach**

Let go of needing to be understood, praised, or validated. You are not here to impress. You are here to **express your truth**.

Closing Thought

The Bhagavad Gita wasn't spoken to a monk in a cave.

It was spoken to a warrior, in crisis, in the middle of chaos.

Your moment of burnout is not a sign of weakness. It is your **invitation to evolve**.

To reframe your ambition.

To recalibrate your actions.

To rise again—not for reward, but for **real alignment**.

When Arjuna rose after the Gita, he wasn't the same warrior.

He had become something greater:

A **conscious instrument of purpose**.

So will you.

CHAPTER 9

DECISION FATIGUE AND EMOTIONAL OVERLOAD

"Even dharma, when pursued without pause, can become a burden."

– On the quiet exhaustion of always doing the right thing

The Thousand Cuts of the Mind

Modern professionals are not short of intelligence.

They are short of **inner space**.

You wake up with messages to answer.

You attend meetings, you barely register.

You make decisions—small, large, and in between—every hour.

And at night, instead of peace, there is more thinking, more fixing, more **processing**.

This is not laziness. It's **mental overload**.

Like Arjuna on the battlefield—paralyzed, not because he didn't know what to do, but because **he had thought too much, felt too deeply, and carried too long**.

This chapter is a return to **resilience**—not as hardening, but as **clarifying**.

It is a path back to balance, where personal and professional dharma's no longer compete, but **co-exist**.

When the Warrior Feels Worn

The Mahabharata shows us heroes in pain:

- Yudhishthira overwhelmed by moral contradictions
- Arjuna immobilized by guilt and grief
- Karna burdened by loyalty and longing
- Draupadi torn between dignity and duty

None of them were weak.

But each of them reached a point where **their emotional tank ran empty**.

Today's version of this looks like:

- Decision fatigue: even choosing dinner feels like a chore
- Compassion burnout: always giving, never replenishing
- Role confusion: Am I a leader, a parent, a healer, a warrior—or all at once?
- Emotional numbness: not because you don't care, but because **you cared too much, too often**

The Mahabharata doesn't just glorify the war.

It teaches **how to pause within it.**

Resilience is Not a Trait—It's a Rhythm

We often think resilience means never falling.

But the Mahabharata redefines it: **resilience is your ability to return**.

After:

- A difficult quarter
- A painful personal season
- A wrong decision
- A burnout phase

Like Bhima, who falls and rises with primal strength.

Like Arjuna, who breaks down only to break through.

Like Krishna, who pauses between wars with flute and silence.

You don't need to be unshakable.

You need to be **re-centerable**.

The Inner Reservoir: Where Clarity Returns

Krishna never tells Arjuna, "Stop feeling."

Instead, he tells him to **look beyond the noise**, to find the part of himself that:

- Is not the role
- Is not the doubt
- Is not the reaction

"You are not this sorrow, Arjuna. You are awareness that observes it."

In practical terms, clarity returns when you:

- Step out of the inbox to breathe
- Take time off not as a luxury, but as a **strategy**
- Journal, reflect, walk without headphones
- Realign your goals not with ambition, but with **inner relevance**

That's when you stop reacting and start responding.

Personal Dharma vs. Professional Dharma

Your professional dharma may ask:

- "Deliver this."
- "Lead that."
- "Be available always."

But your personal dharma may whisper:

- "Rest."
- "Create."
- "Reconnect with your child."
- "Take care of your body."

Both are sacred.

But when one devours the other, **imbalance becomes identity**.

Draupadi continued to play queen and mother even in exile.

Arjuna resumed his warrior role, but only after reclaiming his spirit.

You must ask:

"What role am I over-playing?

What part of me is being ignored in the name of duty?"

Integration is not doing everything perfectly.

It is knowing when to shift roles without guilt or confusion.

Decision Detox: Practical Clarity Habits

To overcome fatigue and regain decision power:

1. **Create Decision-Free Zones** – block time where no choices need to be made (nature walks, meals without screens, etc.)
2. **Ritualize the Small** – automate or simplify daily tasks (outfits, food, etc.) to reduce micro-decisions
3. **Check Your Energy, Not Just Your Calendar** – don't just manage time, manage **emotional bandwidth**
4. **Build Inner Circles of Reflection** – mentors, coaches, or simply a friend who holds space
5. **Let Some Things Be Unfinished** – choose peace over perfection

Because **you don't need to do more—you need to be more present to what you already carry**.

Closing Thought

When you are tired, rest.

When you are confused, pause.

When your dharma feels too heavy, realign—don't abandon.

The Mahabharata shows us that even the greatest warriors **struggled not with enemies—but with exhaustion**.

Victory begins when you learn to stop fighting yourself.

So before your next big decision, before your next leadership leap, ask not just:

"What must I do?"

But also:

"Who must I be to do this well?"

And remember:

True resilience is not how long you endure,

It is **how gently you return**.

PART IV

ABHIMANYU – THE DARING MILLENNIAL LEADER

CHAPTER 10

ABHIMANYU - COURAGE IN THE UNKNOWN

"He knew how to enter the labyrinth, but not how to exit. And still, he chose to enter."

– On the bravery and vulnerability of young brilliance

The Youngest Warrior, the Boldest Leap

Abhimanyu was just sixteen.

He was not supposed to fight on the front lines.

He was not meant to be the game-changer of Day 13 in the Kurukshetra war.

And yet, he walked into the most complicated military formation—the **Chakravyuha**—knowing only how to get in, not how to get out.

He did it because no one else was available.

He did it because time was short and the stakes were high.

He did it because that's what **true potential does—it rises before it's fully ready**.

Abhimanyu symbolizes today's millennial and Gen Z professionals:

- Incredibly intelligent and driven
- Exceptionally bold, hungry for growth
- Emotionally expressive and self-aware
- But also—at risk of being **under-supported and overexposed**

This chapter is a reflection on that spirit: **brave, bright, but burning out too soon**.

The Chakravyuha of Modern Workplaces

Abhimanyu didn't die because he lacked courage.

He fell because he didn't have support.

The Chakravyuha wasn't just a formation—it was a symbol of:

- Complexity
- Closed systems
- Layers of hierarchy
- Politics and deception

Young professionals today walk into their own modern Chakravyuha:

- Fast-growth startups with undefined roles
- Legacy systems demanding innovation without clarity
- Competitive environments that reward speed, not sustainability

They charge ahead because they're passionate.

But many falter not due to lack of skill—but because **no one taught them how to exit**, recover, or recalibrate.

Mentorship Is Not a Luxury. It's a Lifeline.

Abhimanyu knew how to enter the maze because he had heard part of the story in his mother's womb.

He didn't know how to exit because **no one had completed the teaching**.

In today's corporate culture, how often do we:

- Celebrate youth without preparing them for setbacks?
- Assign responsibility without emotional scaffolding?
- Reward outcomes but ignore burnout?

Every Abhimanyu needs:

- A Krishna (strategist)
- A Kunti (nurturer)
- A Partha (peer or brother figure)
- A team that doesn't just watch—but walks with them

Otherwise, we keep creating heroes—only to watch them fall without closure.

Potential Without Process = Fragility

Abhimanyu was powerful. But that power wasn't tempered with experience.

He lacked the tools to:

- Navigate betrayal
- Protect his energy
- Know when to retreat

That's the risk with today's high performers.

We mistake raw output for resilience.

We confuse early success with emotional maturity.

So, when pressure mounts, many:

- Doubt their own worth
- Quit too soon or stay too long
- Crumble silently behind Instagram-perfect lives

Resilience doesn't come from winning—it comes from being **guided through losing**, and still choosing to rise.

What Leaders Must Learn from Abhimanyu's Fall

If you're a leader or organization builder, ask yourself:

- Are we giving space for brilliance *and* boundaries?
- Do we reward courage, but punish failure harshly?
- Are we giving feedback or just assigning deliverables?
- Do we talk about mental well-being, or only about performance?

Young leaders need **psychological safety**, not just professional applause.

They need people who will say:

"It's okay to not know the way out.

Let's figure it out together."

For the Abhimanyu's Reading This

If you are the Abhimanyu—bright, bold, but sometimes overwhelmed—this is for you:

- You don't have to prove your worth in one battle.
- Being fearless is admirable—but being supported is essential.
- Ask for guidance. That's not weakness, it's wisdom.
- You are allowed to pause, retreat, reflect, and return.

Because real leadership isn't just about entry.

It's about **knowing how to navigate complexity while protecting your spirit**.

Closing Thought

Abhimanyu didn't fail.

We failed him—by not being there, not preparing him, not backing him when it mattered most.

Let's stop romanticizing youthful sacrifice.

Let's build ecosystems where young brilliance doesn't burn out, but **burns bright—consistently, sustainably, joyfully**.

So the next time someone walks into their own Chakravyuha—

Don't just admire their courage.

Be their exit strategy.

Because the future of leadership isn't just about bold entry—

It's about **resilient journeys and graceful returns**.

CHAPTER 11

THE HALF-KNOWLEDGE TRAP

"He had courage without completion, knowledge without guidance—and the world praised him until he collapsed."

– On Abhimanyu and the myth of raw potential

The Illusion of Being Ready

Half-knowledge is seductive.

It makes you believe you're fully equipped because:

- You've read enough LinkedIn posts
- You've aced the interviews
- You've watched leaders from a distance

And yet, when complexity hits—suddenly, it's not about your IQ or intent.

It's about navigation, nuance, **and knowing what to do when the known ends**.

Abhimanyu's story is a sharp metaphor:

- He could enter the Chakravyuha (problem), but didn't know the exit (solution pathway)

- He was courageous enough to begin, but lacked the support to **sustain**
- He was applauded for stepping in—but **abandoned** when things got difficult

This is the tragedy of so many bright, young professionals.

They are celebrated for diving into complexity—without being taught how to come out intact.

What Is Half-Knowledge?

Half-knowledge is:

- Knowing how to use tools, but not how to wield wisdom
- Understanding process, but not context
- Acting fast, but without clarity on long-term consequences
- Starting brilliantly, but with no inner muscle to handle resistance or conflict

It isn't a flaw.

It's a **structural failure**—a gap between how we on-board talent and how we sustain it.

Burnout: The Natural Outcome of Incomplete Guidance

Abhimanyu didn't fail because he wasn't skilled.

He failed because:

- The system sent him in too early

- He was isolated when most vulnerable
- His potential was exploited, not protected

Sound familiar?

Young professionals today face:

- Constant visibility but poor mentorship
- High accountability but little autonomy
- The pressure to perform without permission to pause

This leads to:

- Early burnout
- Emotional disconnection
- Imposter syndrome masked by overachievement

You don't need to be incompetent to burn out.

You just need to be unsupported.

The Responsibility of Systems

Workplaces, educational institutions, and even families must ask:

- Are we preparing our Abhimanyus for **depth**, not just speed?
- Are we teaching resilience, or just celebrating deliverables?
- Are we giving emotional skills with technical roles?

The Mahabharata teaches us that talent is not enough.

Without mentors, protectors, and guides—**brilliance collapses on its own sharp edge**.

System design must evolve from:

- Performance-only cultures → Development cultures
- Mentorship-as-afterthought → Mentorship-as-structure
- Individual heroics → Collective resilience

The Mentorship Blueprint

A sustainable organization doesn't just recruit talent.

It builds an **ecosystem for wisdom transfer**.

Here's what that looks like:

1. **Guided Exposure** – Don't throw new hires into the fire. Let them shadow, ask, and understand.
2. **Feedback Without Fear** – Create a space where questioning is not punished but encouraged.
3. **Normalize Vulnerability** – Leaders who share failure stories create safer spaces.
4. **Build Knowledge Ladders** – Teach not just *what* to do, but *why* it matters.
5. **Design Check-Out Mechanisms** – Everyone must know how to **exit complexity with dignity**.

Because the true test of leadership is not who starts—but **who stays whole** while navigating storms.

Young Professionals: How to Avoid the Trap

If you're a young achiever, here's your checklist:

- Don't mistake confidence for capability. Stay curious.
- Ask for context, not just instructions.
- Seek mentors, not just managers.
- Build recovery routines—burnout is not a badge.
- Respect your limits—stepping back is sometimes the most strategic move.

And most importantly:

Refuse to be someone's shortcut.

Your journey deserves depth, not just direction.

Closing Thought

Abhimanyu's story didn't end because he lacked greatness.

It ended because **the system failed to complete his circle**.

We must learn.

Stop glorifying young sacrifice.

Start designing structures that **complete, support, and sustain brilliance**.

Let's ensure that the next Abhimanyu doesn't just enter the battlefield—but emerges stronger, wiser, and whole.

Because potential, when protected, doesn't just survive—it **transforms the world**.

CHAPTER 12

THE LEGACY OF SACRIFICE AND BRAVERY

"Not every legacy must end in loss. Sometimes, bravery is not in dying—it is in ensuring others don't have to."

– On learning from Abhimanyu's sacrifice

The Aftermath of Valour

Abhimanyu died a hero.

The war paused to mourn him.

But mourning is not enough. Legacy demands **reflection**.

Why do we celebrate those who gave everything, but rarely ask—**could that loss have been prevented?**

In corporate life, in families, in start-ups, and social movements—we often mistake sacrifice for strength.

But true leadership doesn't just honour bravery.

It **learns from it**.

This chapter is not a tribute to Abhimanyu's death.

It is a call to ensure **his kind of brilliance doesn't have to die again**.

Setbacks as Seeds of Legacy

Setbacks aren't always mistakes.

Sometimes, they are **mirrors**—showing us:

- The gaps in our systems
- The assumptions in our thinking
- The urgency to evolve

Abhimanyu's fall wasn't just a loss for the Pandavas.

It was a message:

"Don't push the young into complexity without equipping them with clarity, support, and wisdom."

The Mahabharata doesn't hide the pain of his death.

Because some stories are meant to **pierce**, not comfort.

And in that piercing, we find purpose.

Bravery Without Systemic Change Is a Cycle

How many times have we seen this pattern?

- A young leader burns out, and we call it passion

- A startup collapses under its own ambition, and we call it learning
- A social worker gives everything to a cause, and we call it dedication

We glorify these stories.

But if the system doesn't change, **we're just watching the same movie on repeat**, with different actors.

True legacy is when we say:

- "Let's not send the next one in unprepared."
- "Let's question why sacrifice became the norm."
- "Let's create spaces where excellence doesn't need to bleed."

Transforming Pain into Pathways

Abhimanyu's sacrifice must evolve from story into **strategy**.

Here's how:

1. **Capture Learnings from Setbacks**
   Every burnout, every failure—journal it, decode it, discuss it. Use it to improve your system.
2. **Institutionalize Debriefing**
   Create structured time after high-pressure projects to talk openly—what worked, what broke, what was unsaid?
3. **Protect Boldness with Boundaries**
   Don't dim passion—**but create guardrails**. High performers need clarity, not just opportunity.

4. **Normalize Mid-Career Reinvention**
   Allow young professionals to pivot without shame—changing direction is not quitting; it's **intelligent recalibration**.

A New Way to Lead the Young

If you lead teams, remember:

- A legacy leader doesn't just give the mic—they **stay around to teach the tune**
- Don't use high performers as execution tools. Mentor them into thinkers.
- Build capacity, not just dependency
- Challenge young minds—but stay close enough to catch them if they fall

Dronacharya trained Arjuna—but Abhimanyu didn't have that luxury.

Let's make sure no other Abhimanyu fights alone.

For the Brave Ones Still Rising

If you've faced setbacks, this is your truth:

- Your pain wasn't wasted.
- Your effort planted seeds in unseen ways.
- Your experience is someone else's map—**if you share it**.

Leadership doesn't begin with victory.

It begins when you look at your wounds and say:

"I will rise—not just for myself, but to ensure others don't have to fall the same way."

Closing Thought

Bravery is not just in stepping forward.

It is in **staying back long enough to light the way for others**.

Let Abhimanyu's legacy not be a cautionary tale—

Let it be a **turning point**.

A call to every organization, institution, and individual:

Honour sacrifice not with applause, but with change.

Because the true tribute to bravery is not in statues or speeches—

It is in creating systems where the next generation doesn't need to die proving their worth.

They rise, thrive, and carry the legacy forward—**with wholeness, not wounds**.

PART V

BHIMA – THE FORCE OF ACTION AND EMOTIONAL INTELLIGENCE

CHAPTER 13

BHIMA - STRENGTH WITH LOYALTY

"His strength wasn't just muscle—it was moral. He didn't shout about his loyalty. He proved it, again and again."

The Underrated Pillar

In most stories of the Mahabharata, Bhima is typecast—the muscle-bound powerhouse, the angry avenger. But this lens misses his most vital trait: **loyalty that never wavered, even when it was unacknowledged**.

Bhima was not just the Pandavas protector. He was their emotional anchor:

- He carried Draupadi's humiliation as his personal vow.
- He never competed for leadership, yet never stepped back from responsibility.
- Even in times when his rage could have consumed him, he used it to **fuel purposeful action**.

In the modern workplace, Bhima exists in every organization:

The doer. The emotional shield. The team protector.

Often overshadowed by more visible leaders, but always holding the structure together.

Loyalty in the Face of Invisibility

Bhima never demanded validation.

He didn't seek applause when he defended Draupadi or fought Duryodhana.

But behind every Pandavas success stood his tireless strength.

This mirrors team members who:

- Stay late to clean up what others ignore
- Stand up for team morale when no one else will
- Absorb pressure quietly, shielding others from the storm

Leadership isn't always visible. Sometimes it shows up as the **quiet warrior**, always on your side.

Turning Anger into Constructive Fire

Bhima's anger was volcanic—but it had direction.

When Draupadi was insulted, his fury wasn't chaos—it became a **sacred vow**.

Modern leadership demands this kind of discipline:

- To feel deeply, but act with intention
- To stand up against wrong, without becoming destructive

- To use emotion as **fuel**, not as a flame that burns bridges

---

Closing Reflection – Bhima's Silent Leadership

Loyalty is not about being noticed—it's about being **needed**.

True strength is protecting others, even when no one is watching.

As leaders or teammates, we must look for the Bhimas in our teams—those who don't talk the loudest, but **hold the fort**.

And if you are one, never feel small for standing tall in silence.

You are not invisible.

You are **indispensable**.

CHAPTER 14

WHEN EMOTION BECOMES POWER

Emotional Intelligence vs. Impulsiveness

Bhima's Protective Instinct as People Leadership

"He knew rage. He lived through humiliation. But he never let his fire become destruction."

The Emotional Backbone of the Pandavas

In war, Bhima roared.

In love, he softened.

In pain, he stayed silent.

But in all things, Bhima was **authentic**.

Bhima represents a kind of emotional intelligence not found in textbooks:

- He doesn't suppress emotion—he **honours** it
- He doesn't react impulsively—he channels it toward purpose
- He doesn't isolate himself—he carries others emotionally, even when he himself is hurting

In leadership today, we are told to be emotionally "stable"—often a euphemism for *unfeeling*.

But Bhima teaches a more evolved form of leadership:

Emotionally expressed, strategically directed.

People Leadership Begins with Emotional Literacy

Bhima was never the strategist. But he was the protector.

He instinctively:

- Knew when a team member was emotionally shaken
- Reacted to injustice—not for personal ego, but for collective dignity
- Used emotional moments to build **trust**, not just results

People leadership isn't about having all the answers.

It's about being emotionally available **when it matters most**.

Impulse vs. Emotional Power

Yes, Bhima was impulsive at times.

But over the course of the Mahabharata, he transforms—learning to let his anger *breathe before it bursts.*

This is the heart of emotional intelligence:

- Know your triggers
- Pause long enough to choose

- Act with clarity, not charge

And leaders who do this:

- De-escalate tensions before they explode
- Model strength that doesn't rely on domination
- Protect without possessing

Closing Reflection – Bhima's Inner Compass

Emotion is not a liability in leadership.

It is the **heartbeat** of connection, trust, and loyalty.

Bhima shows us that **power without empathy is tyranny**, but **power with empathy becomes legacy**.

In your team, don't just ask: "What are we feeling?"

Ask: "What will we do with these feelings—together?"

Because when emotion becomes power, **people feel seen—and they stay**.

CHAPTER 15

THE WEIGHT OF SILENCE AND THE POWER OF EXPRESSION

Balancing Internal Struggle with External Courage

"Even the strongest need space to fall apart. Bhima bled—but he bled in silence."

What No One Saw in Bhima

We celebrate Bhima's victories.

But we rarely pause to ask: what did he **suppress** to keep others safe?

He:

- Never fully voiced the guilt of not preventing Draupadi's humiliation
- Grieved silently after the loss of his son, Ghatotkacha
- Carried the emotional burden of vengeance without complaint

This is what happens to many **leaders and protectors**:

They feel responsible for everyone else, but are **unseen in their own pain**.

The Strong Suffer Quietly—Until They Break

The problem with silence isn't just that it's lonely.

It's that it **distorts self-worth**.

Bhima began to internalize:

- "My pain doesn't matter."
- "I must always be strong."
- "If I speak, I will disappoint."

This is mirrored in workplaces today where:

- Leaders bottle up for fear of losing respect
- High performers pretend all is well while unravelling inside
- People prioritize **performance over presence**

The danger? **Unaddressed silence leads to unseen burnout**.

Courage Is Expression, Not Just Containment

Eventually, Bhima's vows, actions, and rare expressions become catharsis.

He finds healing in action—but **how much healthier it could have been with honest expression?**

Today, we must:

- Normalize vulnerability in leadership

- Design cultures where **strength and emotion coexist**
- Encourage expression that is safe, not performative

A leader who says, "I'm tired," gives others permission to be **honest**, not **fragile**.

Closing Reflection – Redefining Strength

The strongest are not those who never fall.

They are those who fall, speak, rise, and **keep protecting** with open hearts.

Don't wait for your Bhimas to collapse before you check in.

And if you are Bhima—

- Allow your story to be heard
- Let your fire soften into warmth
- Know that your silence deserves space, but so does your voice

Because your **strength is sacred**, but your **humanity is divine**.

PART VI

ARCHETYPES OF CONFLICT – LESSONS FROM THE FALLEN

CHAPTER 16

YUDHISHTHIRA - THE ETHICAL CEO

"When you are trusted by all, your smallest lie costs the most."

– On the burden of moral leadership

The Crown of Conscience

Yudhishthira, the eldest Pandava, was never the strongest, the fastest, or the most aggressive.

He was the **conscience** of the Pandavas.

He was the one everyone trusted to do what was **right**, even when it wasn't easy.

He didn't lead through charisma or command, but through a **quiet, unwavering integrity**.

In a world of fast decisions, blurred lines, and competitive urgency, Yudhishthira represents the **unshakeable ethical leader**—someone who chooses what is fair, even at personal cost.

The Ethical Dilemma of Modern Leaders

Yudhishthira was not flawless.

He made devastating mistakes—most notably, his decision to gamble away his kingdom, his brothers, and even Draupadi.

And yet, even after losing everything, he did not become cynical. He took responsibility. He chose accountability over ego.

That is his greatness—not his perfection, but his **ability to bear the weight of his choices**.

Modern professionals and leaders face similar tests:

- Do I take responsibility for my team's failure, or do I deflect?
- Do I act in the interest of the project—or protect my reputation?
- Do I give in to the pressure of the board—or hold my values?

Like Yudhishthira, the ethical leader today must carry the **invisible burden of doing what's right when no one is watching**.

When Morality Becomes a Lonely Path

While his brothers burned with rage, Yudhishthira often chose restraint.

- He would not retaliate in Draupadi's sabha.
- He insisted on keeping his word during exile.
- He repeatedly sought peace before war.

To some, this looked like weakness. But it was **strategic forbearance**, rooted in dharma.

In organizations, ethical leaders are often misunderstood:

- They don't make flashy moves.
- They question unfair incentives.
- They raise red flags others ignore.
- They are slow to act, but steady to lead.

It's a lonely path—but a necessary one.

Because **when trust is broken, systems collapse**.

The Cost of Being the Ethical Anchor

Ethical leadership is not just about values. It is about **holding pain without projection**.

Yudhishthira bore:

- The humiliation of his wife.
- The wrath of his brothers.
- The silence of Krishna.
- The inner turmoil of being both king and brother.

Yet he didn't escape his duty.

Leaders today must sometimes:

- Approve decisions they don't like.
- Say "no" to promotions if they compromise fairness.
- Be transparent in times of uncertainty, even when it exposes them.

This is the essence of Yudhishthira: **He didn't just play the role of king. He embodied the soul of the kingdom.**

Truth Is Not Always Absolute

Yudhishthira is famously known for **never lying**—until one fateful day in the war, when Krishna asked him to speak a **half-truth** to mislead Drona.

He reluctantly said:

"Ashwatthama is dead..."

(whispering) "...the elephant."

That day, even truth came with a moral price.

This is the complexity of real-world leadership:

- Sometimes, silence is wiser than speaking.
- Sometimes, short-term deception protects a larger vision.
- Sometimes, you must choose **the least harmful path**, not the perfect one.

Yudhishthira teaches us that ethical leadership is not about being *technically right*—it is about being **existentially responsible**.

The Weight of Dharma

Dharma is not a rulebook. It is a compass.

Yudhishthira spent his life **balancing his personal beliefs with the demands of the world**:

- He honoured his commitments to enemies.
- He forgave when others would take revenge.
- He accepted blame for the war, even when Krishna absolved him.

This wasn't weakness—it was **spiritual strength**.

Young professionals often ask:

- "Can I succeed without compromising?"
- "Can I be good and still be powerful?"

Yudhishthira's life answers: Yes. But **it will cost you**.

And that cost is **consciousness, not compromise**.

Modern-Day Yudhishthiras

In today's world, Yudhishthiras are:

- The CFOs who don't bend accounting to please investors.
- The managers who don't play politics, even if it means slower promotions.
- The entrepreneurs who reject unethical funding to protect integrity.
- The employees who report wrongdoing even when it endangers their own role.

They may not be loud. But they **outlast everyone**.

Why? Because they are **trusted**.

And trust, in a noisy world, is **currency beyond measure**.

Closing Thought

Yudhishthira shows us that **true leadership is not about being celebrated, but being reliable**.

His power was not in aggression, but in **grace under moral pressure**.

He reminds us:

Leadership is not about having all the answers.

It is about having the integrity to question yourself,

and the courage to act anyway.

So when you are tested—when you must choose between ease and ethics—pause and ask:

"What would Yudhishthira do?"

Then choose—not what's easy, not what's fast—but what lets you **sleep with a clear conscience**.

Because when the dust settles, and the titles fade, only one thing remains:

Your inner alignment.

CHAPTER 17

KARNA - THE LOYAL BUT LOST TALENT

"He had everything—courage, skill, generosity. But he craved the one thing he never received: acceptance."

– On Karna's inner conflict

The Outsider Among Giants

Karna is perhaps the most emotionally complex character in the Mahabharata.

- Born a prince, raised by a charioteer.
- As skilled as Arjuna, yet denied his due.
- Loyal to Duryodhana, yet pulled by inner dharma.
- Always on the cusp of greatness, yet **held back by his longing to belong**.

In every high-performing team, there is someone like Karna:

- Supremely capable
- Fiercely loyal
- Operating from a place of deep inner conflict
- Constantly trying to prove their worth

Karna's story is a lens into the **emotional cost of unworthiness**, and how that impacts leadership, decision-making, and legacy.

Loyalty vs. Alignment

Karna's loyalty to Duryodhana is legendary.

After being rejected by society, Duryodhana gave him status, friendship, and validation.

In return, Karna gave everything—even when he knew Duryodhana's path was flawed.

This is where Karna's greatness and tragedy intersect.

Loyalty is beautiful—but when it comes at the cost of **your own truth**, it becomes self-betrayal.

Modern professionals often face the same dilemma:

- Stay with a company that once gave you a break, even if it's now toxic
- Remain loyal to a mentor whose values no longer align with yours
- Stick to a team out of emotional debt, not mutual growth

Karna teaches us this critical question:

Are you loyal to a person—or to your own higher purpose?

The Hunger to Be Seen

At the heart of Karna's journey is **a hunger for recognition**.

Despite his brilliance, he was constantly judged for his birth.

Even his greatest accomplishments came with disclaimers.

This constant rejection created **an inner wound**—one that no title, no amount of generosity, and no battlefield victory could heal.

He needed the world to accept him before he could accept himself.

And that's the lesson:

Validation from outside is unstable currency.

True leadership is built on inner worth, not external applause.

The Weight of Resentment

Resentment fuelled Karna's fire.

He was hurt—but never healed.

He remembered every insult, every slight, and it hardened him.

That fire made him resilient—but also **rigid**.

He refused Krishna's offer of kingship because it came too late.

He refused to leave Duryodhana's side, even after learning his true birthright.

Pride, when mixed with pain, becomes **self-sabotage**.

In leadership today, unresolved emotional wounds often show up as:

- Over defensiveness
- Avoidance of feedback
- Toxic comparison
- Over-commitment to the wrong goals

Karna's life whispers:

You cannot lead from wounds you haven't acknowledged.

Generosity as Overcompensation

Karna was known for his unmatched generosity.

He gave away everything—even his divine armour and earrings.

Even when it hurt him.

This wasn't just virtue—it was also **an unconscious desire to earn worth**.

How many of us overcompensate the same way?

- Saying yes to every task to prove our commitment
- Working late endlessly to be seen as dedicated
- Giving too much to relationships that don't give back

Generosity must come from **abundance**, not **emptiness**.

Otherwise, it's not giving—it's **leaking**.

Why Karna Never Fully Belonged

Despite his talent, Karna always remained on the fringes:

- Not fully accepted by the Kauravas, despite his loyalty
- Denied brotherhood by the Pandavas, despite his bloodline
- Revered by the public, but never *embraced* by the elite

This is the wound of many professionals who feel like **outsiders**:

- First-generation achievers
- Self-made individuals
- Those who rose without legacy or networks

Karna's arc shows that talent can win wars, but **belonging requires inner healing**.

You may never change how the world sees you.

But you can choose how you see yourself.

What Karna Teaches Every Professional

- **Loyalty is sacred**—but not at the cost of your dharma.
- **You can be brilliant and still feel broken**—honour both.
- **Recognize your wounds**—but don't let them define your worth.
- **Don't confuse validation with alignment**—what you *want* and what is *right* are not always the same.
- **Choose causes that elevate your soul**, not just your status.

Closing Thought

Karna died with glory, but also with **regret**.

He never fully used his brilliance for the cause of truth—because he never truly forgave the world for not recognizing him.

His story is not just of a fallen hero.

It is a mirror held to all of us who sometimes lead from fear of exclusion, or pride masked as loyalty.

May you not have to earn your place by bleeding endlessly.

May you not confuse suffering for strength.

And when the time comes to choose between staying loyal to pain or rising toward truth—

May you choose truth. Even if it means walking alone for a while.

Because the world doesn't need perfect heroes.

It needs **whole humans**, leading from awareness, not abandonment.

CHAPTER 18

DURYODHANA - THE EGOIST IN POWER

"He fought the world, not because it wronged him, but because it didn't agree with him."

– On the tragedy of Duryodhana

The Shadow Leader

Duryodhana was not without talent.

He was charismatic, resourceful, politically sharp, and fiercely loyal to his allies.

And yet, he is remembered not for what he built, but for how he **refused to let go**.

His downfall was not due to lack of power.

It was due to **the illusion of invincibility**.

Every organization has its Duryodhana energy:

- The individual who confuses seniority with superiority
- The leader who surrounds themselves with flattery, not truth
- The talented performer who resents every rising peer

- The professional who believes the system owes them success

Duryodhana teaches us what **not to become**—a cautionary figure for professionals who lead from ego instead of alignment.

The Anatomy of Entitlement

Duryodhana believed the kingdom was his birthright.

It didn't matter that Yudhishthira was more competent or that the elders favoured the Pandavas.

He believed he was wronged—and this belief became his identity.

In modern terms, this is **entitlement syndrome**:

- "I've been here the longest, so I deserve the role."
- "I work the hardest, why don't they recognize me?"
- "I've always delivered—why should I answer to anyone?"

Entitlement breeds comparison, resentment, and eventually, **isolation**.

Duryodhana was surrounded by people—but his decisions were **validated only by echoes**, never by truth.

The Echo Chamber Trap

What fuelled Duryodhana's downfall wasn't just his ego—but his inner circle:

- Shakuni, the manipulator

- Karna, loyal but emotionally wounded
- Dushasana, blindly obedient

Duryodhana never allowed **dissent**, only **consent**.

He chose loyalty over wisdom, obedience over reflection.

In professional life:

- Leaders who surround themselves with yes-men fall into **narrative traps**.
- They hear what they want, not what they **need**.
- They push away talent that challenges them and reward those who play it safe.

Such cultures implode from within.

Why Duryodhana Refused to Evolve

Unlike Arjuna, who paused to reflect, Duryodhana **never questioned himself**.

Even when Krishna offered him peace, he rejected it with pride:

"I will not give the Pandavas even a needlepoint of land."

That line marks the difference between a **conflicted leader** and a **closed one**.

Self-awareness is the beginning of evolution.

Duryodhana had none.

He confused **stubbornness for strength**, **rigidity for righteousness**.

In today's terms, this is the leader who:

- Refuses feedback
- Denies accountability
- Sees change as a threat, not an opportunity
- Prioritizes control over collaboration

Power Without Purpose Is Dangerous

Duryodhana had the army. The allies. The palace.

But he had no peace.

His war was not for dharma. It was for **dominance**.

Professionals must beware of achieving **power without inner alignment**. Because without a larger purpose, power turns:

- Into paranoia
- Success into suffocation
- Leadership into tyranny

True influence doesn't come from control—it comes from **contribution**.

The Redemption That Never Came

What makes Duryodhana's story tragic is not his defeat.

It's that he **never allowed himself to grow**.

Even at death, lying broken, he glorified his choices:

"I have lived like a king, and I die like a warrior."

No introspection. No transformation.

Just a refusal to see that **he was the architect of his ruin**.

Contrast this with Arjuna, who questioned everything—even Krishna.

Or Karna, who, despite his flaws, had moments of deep self-awareness.

Duryodhana shows us that **ego blocks evolution**.

And **entitlement resists reflection**.

Avoiding the Duryodhana Within

We all carry fragments of Duryodhana—moments where:

- We demand without contribution
- We resist feedback
- We hold grudges too long
- We believe we're always right

The key is to **catch the pattern before it becomes identity**.

Ask:

- Do I invite honest feedback, or just validation?
- Can I separate my position from my ego?
- Am I leading from contribution—or compensation for inner insecurity?

- Is there someone I've made a villain just because they don't agree with me?

These questions are your antidote to Duryodhana.

Creating Cultures That Prevent Duryodhanas

Organizations too, must self-reflect:

- Are we rewarding performance over humility?
- Are we creating environments where dissent is punished?
- Are we tolerating brilliance without character?

If yes, we're breeding not leaders—but **cracks in the system**.

Because where Duryodhanas rise, **Krishnas withdraw**.

Closing Thought

Duryodhana was not born evil.

He was born with choices.

He chose to **cling**, not change.

Let his story not scare us—but awaken us.

Because the greatest leadership risk is not failure.

It is **refusing to grow while appearing successful**.

In your journey, remember:

Arjuna doubted and evolved.

Bhima raged and waited.

Abhimanyu lacked guidance, but still rose.

But Duryodhana? He **never paused. Never questioned. Never changed.**

And that's what made him lose—even before the war began.

CHAPTER 19

SHAKUNI - THE SCHEMER

"He never lifted a sword. But he orchestrated a war."

– On the power of manipulation when left unchecked

The Master of Invisible Warfare

Shakuni was not a king.

He wasn't even officially part of the ruling class of Hastinapura.

But through words, whispers, and carefully planted seeds of doubt—he **influenced the course of a dynasty**.

He manipulated Duryodhana, humiliated Yudhishthira, engineered Draupadi's disrobing, and ultimately provoked the great war.

All without raising a single weapon.

He represents the **archetype of covert power**—the person in every organization who:

- Doesn't sit in the front row, but controls decisions from the back

- Isn't accountable, but always influential
- Doesn't break rules directly—but **bends the people who make them**

You may not recognize Shakuni in your team until **it's too late**.

What Does Office Manipulation Look Like Today?

Modern Shakuni's thrive in toxic corporate cultures.

They:

- Play favourites behind the scenes
- Twist information to influence decisions
- Undermine team trust subtly ("I heard leadership is unhappy… just FYI")
- Hide behind emotional intelligence to appear supportive—while **engineering conflict**

These individuals **don't attack you directly**.

They plant the landmines and let others step on them.

And the tragedy?

They often escape consequences, while the organization bleeds.

Why Do Manipulators Thrive?

Because we reward:

- Influence over integrity

- Charisma over clarity
- Silence over confrontation

Shakuni understood systems better than values.

He knew that people often prefer a manipulative ally to a transparent critic.

In many offices, silence is taken as peace—even when it hides war.

Countering Covert Hostility: What the Pandavas Missed

Yudhishthira trusted the system.

He thought reason and righteousness would protect him.

But Shakuni didn't play by those rules.

The Mahabharata teaches:

Even dharma needs discernment.

To counter manipulation in modern workspaces, leaders must:

1. **Listen for patterns, not just incidents** – Manipulators rarely leave clear evidence. Watch **repeated impact**.
2. **Build circles of honest feedback** – Create spaces where people can speak up without fear.
3. **Call out strategy cloaked as support** – The "I'm just being helpful" manipulator must be gently but **firmly unmasked**.
4. **Define ethical boundaries early** – Don't wait until manipulation poisons the culture.

Because what Shakuni thrives on most is **ambiguity**—in values, vision, and voice.

Protecting Yourself in Political Environments

If you feel like you're dealing with a modern-day Shakuni:

- **Don't mirror the manipulation** – It's tempting to fight slyness with slyness. Don't. It will compromise your integrity.
- **Document facts, not feelings** – Keep a record of interactions and impact. Truth must be trackable.
- **Build alliances of clarity** – You don't need everyone to like you. You need the right people to trust you.
- **Stay rooted in values, not vibes** – Office politics feed off emotional overreaction. Detach. Stay precise. Let your actions speak louder.

How to Lead When a Shakuni Is in the Room

If you're in a position of influence, your role is not to **eliminate politics** (they'll always exist).

Your role is to **protect clarity, courage, and conscience**.

Ask:

- Are decisions transparent?
- Is feedback open and reciprocal?
- Are we mistaking cleverness for competence?

Leadership is not just about strategic decisions.

It's about **protecting the culture** from corrosion.

Closing Reflection – What Shakuni Teaches Us

Manipulators rise when good people stay quiet.

They fall when organizations choose courage over comfort.

Shakuni lost in the end—not because the Pandavas outwitted him, but because **the weight of his own deception turned against him**.

The Mahabharata reminds us that **truth has its own timing**.

But we don't need to wait for war to correct what words can clarify.

So the next time you see a Shakuni in your midst:

- Don't fear him
- Don't mirror him
- **Outlast him—with clarity, community, and calm**

Because the best antidote to manipulation is not confrontation—it is **consciousness**.

CHAPTER 20

DRAUPADI – THE VOICE OF DIGNITY AND JUSTICE

"I was dragged, not defeated. My voice shook the heavens because I never lowered it."

– On Draupadi's fierce grace

More Than a Queen

Draupadi was not just a queen.

She was fire incarnate—born from sacrifice, not womb.

She was not built for silence.

She was built to **question, to challenge, and to endure with dignity**.

In the Mahabharata, Draupadi is among the most complex, compelling figures.

She is not passive. She does not conform. She does not forgive easily.

But most importantly—**she never loses her self-respect**, even when stripped of everything else.

Her story resonates powerfully with every professional—especially women—who have ever been:

- Undermined despite excellence
- Objectified or tokenized
- Asked to stay quiet in the face of injustice
- Expected to “endure” for the greater good

The Sabha: Where Humiliation Met Defiance

The turning point in Draupadi’s life—and in the Mahabharata—is the infamous dice game.

She is dragged into the royal court, disrobed, laughed at, and insulted while **elders remain silent** and even her own husbands **look down in shame**.

Yet, she does something no one expects:

She **speaks.**

She **questions.**

She **challenges the legitimacy** of the game, the right of her husbands to stake her, and the silence of the wise.

This is more than rage.

This is **resistance with intelligence**.

She doesn’t collapse. She confronts.

And in doing so, she **breaks centuries of conditioned silence**.

The Professional Parallel: When You're Outnumbered, Not Out voiced

In modern professional spaces, Draupadi moments happen more often than we acknowledge:

- In meetings where credit is stolen
- In workplaces where harassment is ignored
- In environments where leadership dismisses emotional labour
- In cultures where women are expected to stay "likeable" rather than vocal

Draupadi's story reminds us:

Dignity is not preserved by silence.

It is protected by truth spoken at the right moment,

even if it shakes the room.

Her Power Was Her Question

Draupadi's most revolutionary act was not revenge.

It was a **question**.

"Whom did Yudhishthira lose first—himself or me?"

This was not mere logic. It was philosophy, law, and dharma rolled into one.

Her question halted the sabha.

It **exposed the corruption of the game**.

It **shamed the silent**.

It **forced even the powerful to re-evaluate their righteousness**.

In today's world, questions like:

- "Why is this policy unfair to working mothers?"
- "Why is my appraisal lower despite equal contribution?"
- "Why is loyalty expected but not rewarded?"

These are not complaints.

They are **acts of courage**.

Draupadi teaches us that power is not in position—it is in the **fearlessness of articulation**.

Pain Without Bitterness

Despite the humiliation, despite the injustice, Draupadi does not allow herself to become small or petty.

Yes, she vows vengeance.

Yes, she remembers every wound.

But she **does not let her pain define her entirely**.

She continues to walk with the Pandavas, advise them, and be a pillar of their dignity.

This is **resilient grace**.

In professional terms:

- You can be deeply hurt and still hold your head high
- You can feel disillusioned, but still not give up on your principles
- You can carry anger without becoming angry as a person

Draupadi reminds us: **To burn is not to be consumed.**

The Fire That Refused to Dim

Throughout the exile, Draupadi never lets the men forget:

- What happened to her was wrong
- What happened in that court was everyone's failure
- Silence is complicity

She is not bitter. She is **awake**.

This makes her not just a survivor—but a **spiritual strategist**.

She channels her pain into **clarity**, not chaos.

She does not let her trauma define her, but she never forgets it either.

In her, we find the blueprint of **empowered resistance**.

What Draupadi Teaches Every Professional

Whether you are navigating a toxic workplace, battling gender bias, or struggling to be heard:

- Speak—especially when it feels inconvenient
- Question—especially when others stay silent
- Hold your boundary—especially when it's expected to blur
- Own your dignity—especially when others try to take it

Draupadi doesn't ask to be liked. She demands to be respected.

She doesn't let tradition silence her. She **redefines what tradition must become**.

Closing Thought

Draupadi was not a victim.

She was a **witness**, a **warrior**, and ultimately, a **force of change**.

She reminds us:

"You don't have to become the fire.

You already are the fire.

Just stop apologizing for your flame."

In your workplace, your family, your society—when the time comes, and the silence grows loud, may you channel your inner Draupadi:

Graceful. Relentless. Untouched. Undeniable.

PART VII

STRATEGIES TO WIN YOUR WAR – APPLIED WISDOM FOR PROFESSIONALS

CHAPTER 21

TEAM PANDAVAS – BUILDING PURPOSE-LED TEAMS

Trust, Diversity, Ego Management

Collaboration Under Pressure

"They weren't perfect. But they trusted each other through war, exile, silence, and storms."

– On building powerful teams through purpose, not just people

---

A Team Not Chosen, But Forged

The Pandavas were not a conventional team.

They didn't apply for roles.

They were born into their roles, each unique—often conflicting—but bound by a **larger dharma**.

Let's revisit this team:

- **Yudhishthira** – calm, principled, slow but steady
- **Bhima** – action-driven, emotionally charged, deeply loyal

- **Arjuna** – skilled, introspective, prone to emotional highs and lows
- **Nakula & Sahadeva** – quiet specialists, observant, highly intelligent but low profile
- **Draupadi** – emotionally intelligent, politically aware, fiercely resilient
- **Krishna** – strategist, conscience, the unseen force guiding them all

This wasn't a "perfect" team.

It was a **purpose-led collective**, rooted in trust, mutual respect, and a shared mission.

What Makes a Purpose-Led Team Work?

1. **Clarity of Purpose**
   The Pandavas were not fighting for land—they were fighting to **restore dharma**.
   Without clarity of *why*, teams lose coherence during storms.
2. **Trust in Diversity**
   Yudhishthira never tried to make Bhima like Arjuna.
   Draupadi respected Nakula's silence as much as Krishna's voice.
   Each member led in their own way—**difference wasn't feared, it was woven in**.
3. **Managing Ego Without Erosion of Identity**
   Arjuna was proud, Bhima was fiery, and Yudhishthira could be rigid.

But no one let ego derail the mission.
They **realigned**, especially under Krishna's subtle influence.

4. **Space to Shine and Step Back**
Not everyone leads every battle.
In the Pandavas' journey, leadership rotated—Arjuna in war, Yudhishthira in counsel, Draupadi in diplomacy.
Shared leadership strengthens resilience.

Modern Lessons from Team Pandava

In corporate life, building high-performing teams isn't about finding identical mindsets.

It's about:

- **Recruiting for values**, not just skill
- **Respecting unique voices**, even if they don't dominate meetings
- Creating **psychological safety**, so that even a Sahadeva feels heard
- Having a **"Krishna" role**—someone who anchors the team with strategic vision and moral clarity

Team Pandavas is proof that with the right glue—**trust, mission, and space**—diverse people can win even the most complex battles.

How to Build Your Pandavas Team?

1. **Define Your Shared Dharma**
   What does your team stand for beyond quarterly goals?
   A shared "why" powers long-term performance.
2. **Play to Individual Strengths**
   Stop forcing Bhimas to be Arjunas.
   Don't overlook Nakulas because they're quiet.
   Know your people—and let them shine in their roles.
3. **Create Systems for Ego Check**
   Conflict is natural. What matters is how it's processed.
   Use peer reviews, anonymous feedback, and regular alignment sessions.
4. **Build Under Pressure, Not Just in Retreats**
   Anyone can be a good team on a good day.
   But can your team **hold the line** when things go south?

The Pandavas fought for 18 days under blood, betrayal, and personal loss—and still stood aligned.

Signs You Have a Purpose-Led Team

- Members challenge ideas, not people
- Success is shared; failure is processed without blame
- Diversity is seen as an advantage, not an inconvenience
- Loyalty is earned, not enforced
- Silence is respected, not ignored
- The mission survives even if the team is tested

Closing Reflection – The Pandavas Blueprint

A great team is not defined by harmony, but by **how it moves through disharmony**.

The Pandavas argued, doubted, and stumbled—but **never abandoned each other**.

They disagreed without dissolving, suffered without disconnecting, and **rose together**.

In your organization, don't search for the perfect team.

Build the right one.

One that:

- Holds space for difference
- Moves with shared vision
- And, like the Pandavas, can **survive exile and still come back stronger**

Because in the end, the war is not won by the most talented team.

It's won by the one **bound by truth, trust, and timeless commitment**.

CHAPTER 22

CONFLICT MANAGEMENT THE EPIC WAY

"Not every battle was fought on the battlefield. The greatest wars began in silence, sharpened in words, and only then ended in swords."

– On the strategy behind every Mahabharata conflict

The Inevitability of Conflict

Where there are people, there is disagreement.

But conflict is not failure. It is **feedback**.

In the Mahabharata, conflict wasn't a deviation from the path—it was **part of the journey**.

The epic teaches us that:

- Conflict ignored becomes karma
- Conflict misunderstood becomes chaos
- Conflict addressed with clarity becomes **growth**

So the question isn't *how to avoid conflict*, but *how to manage it consciously*.

Root-Cause Clarity: See Beneath the Surface

When Duryodhana plotted against the Pandavas, the reason wasn't just jealousy—it was fear of losing power.

When Karna joined the Kauravas, the issue wasn't hatred—it was his **need for dignity and belonging**.

Too often in teams and organizations, we:

- Fight over symptoms, not causes
- Attack people, not patterns
- React to words, not the emotions underneath

To manage conflict like the Mahabharata, you must ask:

- What is this really about?
- Whose identity, security, or purpose feels threatened here?
- What's the unspoken fear beneath this visible friction?

This is **root-cause clarity**—the first principle of epic conflict management.

Three Conflict Strategies from the Mahabharata

1. Diplomacy: The Wisdom of Krishna

Before the war, Krishna didn't pick up a bow.

He went on a **peace mission**.

He listened to both sides, sought compromise, and offered solutions.

"Give them five villages," he told Duryodhana. "Avoid war."

Diplomacy isn't weakness. It is a **strategic restraint**.

Apply it when:

- Emotions are raw
- Stakes are high
- Long-term relationships matter more than short-term wins

Modern Tip: Use active listening, neutral facilitation, and values-based negotiation. Let everyone feel seen before they can shift position.

2. Confrontation: The Strength of Draupadi and Bhima

Not all conflict can be resolved through softness.

When Draupadi was insulted in court, she confronted the silence.

Bhima made his vows in the open. They **named the injustice**.

"A vow spoken aloud is a compass under pressure."

Sometimes, silence is complicity.

Sometimes, truth must be spoken into uncomfortable rooms.

Use confrontation when:

- Boundaries are being violated
- Justice is being compromised

- Delay is empowering the aggressor

Modern Tip: Confront behaviour, not people. Set boundaries with clarity, not cruelty. Document. Stay values-aligned, not emotion-fuelled.

3. Timing: The Intelligence of Yudhishthira

Yudhishthira knew **when to wait**.

He bore insult after insult, knowing the time was not yet right.

He gathered allies, watched dynamics, and played the long game.

"A wrong response at the right time can be forgiven. A right response at the wrong time can be fatal."

Great leaders know:

- When to speak
- When to pause
- When to let others lead

Conflict resolution is not just about what you do. It's about **when** you do it.

Modern Tip: Before reacting, assess timing. Is the system ready? Is the team emotionally receptive? Is escalation a path to solution—or to ego warfare?

The Conflict Triangle: A Simple Framework

When conflict arises in a team, ask yourself:

1. **What's the root cause?**
   (Power? Belonging? Uncertainty?)

2. **Which approach fits?**
   (Diplomacy? Confrontation? Strategic delay?)
3. **What's the right timing?**
   (Now, or after stabilizing?)
   Overlaying Mahabharata wisdom on modern conflict turns chaos into **clarity**.

Leadership Responsibility in Conflict

As a leader, your job is not to eliminate disagreement.

Your job is to:

- Create **structures** for healthy disagreement
- Discourage political triangulation
- Protect truth-tellers without punishing question-askers
- Separate **emotion from action**, but not empathy from listening

True leaders don't rush into every fire.

They **stand at the center** and cool the system from within.

Closing Reflection – Win Without War

The Mahabharata teaches us that **every war was preceded by a chance to avoid it**.

Conflict is rarely fatal—but ignorance of its roots is.

Don't suppress conflict. Don't fear it.

Decode it. Design around it. Discuss it.

Sometimes your team needs a Krishna.

Sometimes it needs a Bhima.

But always—it needs a **Yudhishthira** to hold the moral compass, and say:

"We will not destroy each other to win this."

Because in the real Kurukshetra, the battle is not between people.

It is between **ego and evolution**.

Between **reaction and responsibility**.

Choose your strategy. Choose your timing.

And **win your war without losing your people**.

CHAPTER 23

THE ART OF WITHDRAWAL - LESSONS FROM EXILE

Why Stepping Back Can Be Powerful

Reflection, Reset, and Inner Mastery

"Sometimes you win not by charging ahead, but by learning how to pause with purpose."

– On the Pandavas' exile and the strategy of stillness

Exile: A Time of Defeat or Redesign?

The Pandavas' thirteen-year exile is often seen as a punishment.

But spiritually and strategically, it was a time of **deep transformation**.

During exile:

- **Arjuna** acquired divine weapons through intense discipline
- **Yudhishthira** mastered inner calm and philosophical wisdom
- **Bhima** sharpened his emotional control

- **Draupadi** rediscovered her voice in solitude
- Even **Krishna**, though not in exile, used this period to **build alliances and prepare for war**

Their physical absence from the kingdom wasn't passivity.

It was **a strategic withdrawal**—not to escape, but to **emerge stronger**.

In today's world, we must reframe withdrawal not as weakness—but as **the highest form of wisdom**.

Why Stepping Back Can Be Powerful

In professional life, the pressure to stay visible, productive, and in motion is relentless.

But growth doesn't always happen in the spotlight.

Modern "exile" can take many forms:

- A sabbatical
- A career break
- A pause after burnout
- Stepping back from leadership to realign values
- Saying "no" to a toxic environment, even without a clear next step

And in that silence, if used wisely, you gain:

- Clarity of vision
- Strength of will

- Mastery over ego
- A reconnection with your core purpose

The silence between chapters is what gives meaning to the story.

Three Lessons from the Pandava Exile

1. Reflection Is Not Inactivity

The Pandavas didn't just sit in the forest and mourn.

They read scriptures, trained their bodies, and deepened their wisdom.

Arjuna didn't waste time blaming Duryodhana—he went inward and upward.

In your withdrawal phase:

- Reflect, don't ruminate
- Ask: What did I miss in the noise?
- Journal, meditate, walk alone—**let clarity return to the surface**

Modern Tip: Schedule time to **disconnect to reconnect**. Use silence as a strategy, not as a reaction.

---

2. Reset Your Inner Operating System

When you're deep in battle mode, you operate on reflex.

Exile teaches you to shift from **reaction to reflection**.

Ask:

- What patterns no longer serve me?
- What does success mean for me now?
- Where is my energy most alive?

The Pandavas didn't come out of exile as the same people.

They came out **evolved**—ready to win not just with weapons, but with wisdom.

Modern Tip: Use this time to unlearn false urgency. Design your life to prioritize alignment over achievement.

---

3. Re-Enter with Purpose, Not Pressure

When their exile ended, the Pandavas didn't rush into war.

They sent Krishna as a peace envoy first.

They used strategy, not emotion, to engage the battlefield.

Similarly, when you return from a professional withdrawal:

- Don't jump back into old patterns
- Re-enter on **your terms**, with **renewed boundaries** and **clarity**
- Rebuild intentionally, not reactively

Your re-entry is your **rebirth**.

The Ego Trap of Relentless Action

Why do we resist stepping back? Because:

- We fear being forgotten
- We think rest is laziness
- We associate stillness with irrelevance

But this is the voice of the **untrained ego**.

The Mahabharata shows us: **true warriors don't always fight**.

They know when to **pause, prepare, and rise again**.

Redefining Productivity Through Stillness

What if we started seeing:

- Sabbaticals as leadership training?
- Rest as resilience practice?
- Stillness as a professional superpower?

Then the withdrawal wouldn't feel like exile.

It would feel like **refinement**.

In a culture obsessed with hustle, **the brave ones choose healing**.

Closing Reflection – The Sacred Pause

You do not become less valuable when you step back. You become more rooted.

The tree doesn't grow in spring—it survives in winter.

Exile gave the Pandavas more than just time—it gave them **transcendence**.

In your life, know when to fight…

And just as importantly, know when to **retreat with reverence**.

Because in that retreat, you will:

- Find yourself
- Sharpen your vision
- Return with a power no storm can shake

That is not withdrawal.

That is **warriorhood in its most sacred form**.

CHAPTER 24

THE ROLE OF THE CONSCIENCE KEEPER – BEING THE KRISHNA IN THE ROOM

Guiding Without Controlling

The Power of Presence, Discernment, and Influence

> *"He never picked up a weapon, but he turned the tide of war."*
>
> **— On Krishna's leadership without command**

Not All Leaders Sit on Thrones

Krishna was never the king of Hastinapura.

He did not command armies, chase credit, or claim political control.

But he was the **moral centre**, the unseen strategist, and the emotional compass for the Pandavas.

In modern professional teams, this is the role of the **conscience keeper**—the person who:

- Grounds decisions in ethics
- Sees beyond ego conflicts
- Guides without spotlight
- **Anchors the team when others drift**

Every team needs a Krishna.

And at some point, **you** will be called to become one.

Who Is the Conscience Keeper in a Team?

The conscience keeper is not always the CEO.

It could be:

- The senior analyst who calls out a bias others miss
- The manager who protects integrity when others push shortcuts
- The peer who calms emotional spirals during chaos
- The person who **asks the question everyone avoids**

They lead not through **authority**, but through **alignment**.

They are often:

- Calm in conflict
- Wise in silence
- Sharp with timing
- Humble, but unshakably anchored in their values

The Three Pillars of Krishna's Leadership

1. Strategic Silence and Timely Speech

Krishna didn't speak in every debate.

But when he did, his words realigned destinities.

"The wise do not react. They respond."

He knew:

- When to listen
- When to ask questions
- When to challenge a decision
- And most importantly—when to let others arrive at their own truth

Modern Insight: If you're a conscience keeper, speak when it matters most. Your words carry **moral weight**, not just noise.

---

2. Influence Without Control

Krishna didn't fight Arjuna's battles for him.

He guided him.

Through questions, reminders, provocations, and presence.

He used **nudge over command**, and **insight over instruction**.

The conscience keeper never says, "Do it because I said so."

They say, "Does this align with what we stand for?"

They restore **inner clarity**, not impose external control.

Modern Insight: Don't fix people. Help them see. Let them rise on their own terms—with your quiet hand behind the scenes.

---

3. Vision Without Attachment

Krishna knew that even his efforts could not stop the war if people chose ego.

He offered clarity.

He offered alternatives.

He prepared Arjuna for all possibilities—including loss.

The conscience keeper understands:

- You are responsible for the **input**, not the **outcome**
- Your role is to serve dharma, not dominate the result
- When it's time to let go, **do so with grace and faith**

Modern Insight: Detach from control. Lead with clarity. Release the results.

How to Be the Krishna in the Room

1. **Cultivate Inner Clarity First**
   You cannot be a conscience keeper if you are unclear inside. Build a practice—reflection, meditation, silence, journaling—whatever keeps your inner compass sharp.
2. **Don't Force, Influence**
   Plant questions, not orders. Offer perspectives, not pressure.
3. **Be Anchored, Not Aggressive**

You don't need to win every argument. You need to **hold the ground of dharma**, even if others fluctuate.

4. **Be Available, Not Always Visible**
   True conscience keepers don't need the spotlight. Their power lies in **presence, not position**.

When the Room Has No Krishna

Many teams fall into dysfunction not because of a lack of intelligence, but a lack of **ethical guidance**.

If there's no one asking:

- "Is this the right thing?"
- "Are we reacting or responding?"
- "What would long-term wisdom say?"

Then performance may rise—but at the **cost of the soul**.

Being the Krishna in the room may not make you the most popular.

But it will make you **the most remembered**—especially when the storms hit.

Closing Reflection – The Leader Without a Crown

You don't need a title to lead. You need vision, integrity, and presence.

Krishna teaches us that the greatest influence is often **subtle, steady, and silent**.

In your family, team, organization, or community, ask:

- "Can I be the one who brings wisdom when emotions take over?"
- "Can I hold space without controlling the room?"
- "Can I keep the focus on dharma—not drama?"

If yes, then you are already walking the path of the **conscience keeper**.

Be the Krishna.

Not because you need to be followed—

But because the world needs more leaders who can stand beside others and say:

"You already know the answer. Let me walk with you until you remember."

CHAPTER 25

REBUILDING AFTER WAR - HEALING AS A LEADERSHIP SKILL

"Winning the war was not the end. It was only the beginning of carrying the cost."

— On what it truly means to lead through recovery

The Forgotten Phase of Leadership

The Mahabharata doesn't end with the Pandavas' victory at Kurukshetra.

It continues — in grief, confusion, and **deep soul-searching**.

After the war:

- **Yudhishthira didn't celebrate**. He collapsed in despair over the bloodshed.
- **Bhima's strength turned to silence**, overwhelmed by the cost of revenge.
- **Arjuna mourned Karna**, finally learning the full story too late.

- **Draupadi, though vindicated, never rejoiced.**

The war was won — but the **soul of the kingdom was fractured**.

This is the phase few leaders are trained for:

Not the execution of strategy, but the **healing of systems and souls**.

Why Healing Is Leadership

After any intense conflict — be it in a project, a merger, an organizational breakdown, or a personal rupture — leaders must pivot from *control* to *care*.

Victory doesn't mean closure.

- Emotions linger
- Distrust simmers
- Fatigue seeps into culture
- The "winners" feel guilt, the "losers" feel unseen

If healing is ignored, dysfunction takes root in silence.

Healing is not "soft."

It is **strategic regeneration** — the act of tending to what is broken so that what is new can grow.

Three Dimensions of Leadership Healing

1. Emotional Debriefing

Post-conflict, the human system needs to **make sense of what happened**.

In the Mahabharata:

- Yudhishthira sought truth from sages
- Krishna consoled the grieving women of Hastinapura
- Dialogues with Bhishma on his deathbed became a **leadership curriculum**

Modern Application:

- Hold post-project retrospectives that aren't just about KPIs — but about *people*
- Acknowledge sacrifices, tensions, and overlooked pain
- Let silence be honoured — not rushed over

People don't heal through deadlines. They heal through **recognition**.

---

2. Rebuilding Trust

War — or any prolonged conflict — creates fractures in trust.

To rebuild:

- Leaders must **own the role they played**, even indirectly
- Apologies (when due) must be offered — not performatively, but **with sincerity**

- Future behaviour must demonstrate change — not just in speeches, but in **systems**

Trust is not rebuilt by saying "we're okay now."

It is rebuilt when **actions match intentions over time.**

Karna might have been on the "wrong" side, but he was not evil. And Arjuna's final grief showed that trust and regret often live side by side.

---

3. Redefining the Culture

After every rupture, culture **shifts**. Leaders can either let that happen by accident or shape it intentionally.

Ask:

- What will we carry forward from this conflict?
- What must we leave behind?
- What new norms must now guide us?

In the post-Kurukshetra era, Yudhishthira became a **philosopher-king**, focused not on expansion, but on ethical governance.

The war had changed him. And his leadership **matured into stewardship**.

Modern Insight: Don't go back to "business as usual." Use the pain as compost for a wiser, healthier work environment.

Signs That a Team Has Healed

- Honest conversations are possible again
- Disagreements happen with respect, not fear
- People speak with hope, not hesitation
- The language of blame is replaced with the language of **learning**
- Even those who left are spoken of with **dignity**, not dismissal

---

Your Role as a Healing Leader

To be a healing leader, you don't need to be everyone's therapist.

But you must be:

- **Present** enough to notice unspoken pain
- **Brave** enough to name the cost of war
- **Humble** enough to admit where you too, were human
- **Patient** enough to wait for reconciliation to grow organically

Healing is not about fixing people. It's about **creating the conditions** in which people can fix themselves — together.

Closing Reflection – The Kingdom After the War

True leadership doesn't end with victory. It begins with humility.

Krishna left the battlefield before the coronation.

He knew: his role was not to rule, but to **guide until the healing began**.

If you've led through conflict — large or small — don't rush past the pain.

Hold space. Breathe. Rebuild.

Let your legacy be not that you won the war,

But that **you taught your people how to live again**.

Because the world doesn't just need conquerors.

It needs **compassionate rebuilders** — leaders who know that:

The greatest power is not in commanding troops, but in restoring hearts.

CHAPTER 26

DAILY KURUKSHETRA PRACTICES

"Even Arjuna, the greatest warrior, began his battle by sitting down and listening within."

– On the power of daily inner work to face outer challenges

Why Daily Discipline Matters in Modern Life

Kurukshetra isn't a one-time battle.

It's daily.

- You wake up to choices — some urgent, some ethical
- You navigate ego, emotion, ambition, and alignment
- You manage teams, expectations, deadlines, and doubt
- And most of all — you deal with yourself

The outer battlefield changes.

But the **inner discipline to respond with clarity** — that's what defines a leader.

This chapter offers **9 practical daily habits** — drawn from the spirit of the Mahabharata, modern psychology, and spiritual wisdom — to help you lead with dharma, not just deliverables.

The 9 Inner Practices of a Daily Kurukshetra Warrior

---

1. Morning Stillness (5–10 minutes of silence)

"Before Arjuna picked up his bow, he sat in silence and listened to Krishna."

Start your day not with your phone — but with your **Self.**

Sit. Breathe. Watch your thoughts. Listen inwardly.

No goal. Just presence.

Why?

Because you can't lead others if you're lost in yourself.

---

2. Intention-Setting

"What is the dharma I must uphold today?"

Write down 1–3 clear intentions:

- What kind of leader do I want to be today?
- What values will guide my choices?
- Where must I be courageous, not comfortable?

Tip: Use simple affirmations like:

- "I choose clarity over confusion."
- "I lead with truth, not fear."
- "I honour my word — and my silence."

---

3. Dharmic Decision Filter

Before acting, ask yourself:

- Is this action aligned with **my core values**?
- Will it cause harm, or bring harmony?
- Am I reacting from fear or responding from clarity?

This becomes your **inner Krishna** — whispering before you speak, sign, or send.

---

4. The Pause Practice

"Krishna didn't rush Arjuna. He paused the entire war for one conversation."

Before difficult conversations, decisions, or responses:

- Take 3 conscious breaths
- Pause your mind's default
- Return to intention

In the pause, wisdom enters.

---

5. Midday Reset (2–3 minutes)

At midday — stop.

Step away from your screen.

Close your eyes. Ask:

- Am I aligned with my morning intention?

- What emotion is driving me right now?
- What do I need to release?

This practice **brings you back to the centre**.

---

6. Journal the Kurukshetra Within

At day's end, ask:

- What battle did I fight today — and what did I learn?
- Where did I act from ego?
- Where did I stay in dharma?

Don't judge. Just witness.

Write it down. This is **your Bhagavad Gita** in progress.

---

7. Gratitude and Release

Before sleep, offer thanks — not for perfection, but for presence.

Thank:

- The challenges that taught you
- The people who triggered your growth
- The mistakes that humbled you

And let the day go. Every battle ends. So must yours.

---

8. The Evening Mirror

Look at yourself — literally.

Ask:

- Did I honour the person I want to become today?
- If not, how can I do better tomorrow — gently, not guiltily?

This reflection is **your private Yudhishthira moment** — a truth-telling without drama.

---

9. Weekly Dharma Check-In (Once a week)

Ask yourself:

- Is my current path nourishing my spirit?
- Am I becoming the kind of leader the world needs?
- Where do I need a course correction?

Optional: Share this with a mentor, therapist, or trusted peer — your **Krishna**.

Daily Template Example

Morning

- ☐ 5 mins silence
- ☐ Write 3 intentions
- ☐ Ask: "What is my dharma today?"

Midday

- ☐ Pause + Breathe + Reflect
- ☐ Emotional check-in

Evening

- ☐ Journaling: Today's battle
- ☐ Mirror Question
- ☐ Gratitude + Letting Go

Closing Reflection – You Are the Battlefield and the Warrior

Dharma isn't a slogan. It's a discipline.

One that must be chosen — daily.

In the Kurukshetra of your life, no one is going to hand you clarity.

You have to **cultivate it.**

These daily practices are not checkboxes.

They are sacred commitments — to your growth, your integrity, and your inner Krishna.

You won't get them perfect. That's not the point.

The point is to **return. Every day. With honesty. With humility. With courage.**

Because leadership is not a role.

It is a rhythm.

PART VIII

CONCLUSION – BE YOUR OWN KRISHNA AND ARJUNA

CHAPTER 27

KURUKSHETRA WITHIN

"At some point in life, no one will come to guide you. You must become both the guide and the warrior."

– The union of wisdom and will

The Final Battle is Always Within

We began this book in your workplace and in your mind—

with the chaos of stress, ambition, office politics, and burnout.

We explored the battles of ego, fatigue, conflict, and duty.

And we met the archetypes—Krishna, Arjuna, Draupadi, Bhima, Abhimanyu, Shakuni—each offering you a mirror.

But now we end not with a war won—

but with **peace discovered**.

Because real success is not about fighting harder.

It's about becoming wiser.

Krishna and Arjuna Live Within You

- **The Arjuna in you** is the doer. The bold one. The one who doubts, who questions, who struggles with emotions and ethics—yet keeps showing up.
- **The Krishna in you** is the inner witness. The strategist. The calm anchor. The voice that whispers truth, even when your mind is in turmoil.

Together, they are **your perfect inner team.**

You don't have to choose between them.

You must **balance them.**

When Arjuna acts without Krishna, he becomes reactive.

When Krishna advises without Arjuna, there is wisdom but no movement.

The modern leader must be **both**:

- Courageous and conscious
- Fast-moving and still-centered
- Emotionally open and ethically grounded

The Journey from Reaction to Response

Let this book guide you from:

Reaction	→	Response
Stress-driven urgency	→	Intention-led action
Ego-led conflict	→	Dharma-based clarity

Reaction	→	Response
Power games and politics	→	Purpose-driven collaboration
Emotional burnout	→	Emotional intelligence
Overthinking and inaction	→	Inner clarity, outer courage

This is your **Kurukshetra evolution**.

Your Work Is Now Your Ashram

You don't have to escape to the mountains.

Your workplace can be your spiritual ground.

Your boardroom, your battleground.

Your journal, your chariot.

Your breath, your bow.

Your self-awareness—**your Krishna**.

The ancient sages didn't teach escape.

They taught **engagement with awareness**.

Now, in your meetings, deadlines, and dilemmas,

ask:

"What would my Krishna say here?"

"How would Arjuna act with clarity, not confusion?"

Because the ultimate evolution is not external success.

It is **internal alignment**.

You Are Now the Storyteller

The Mahabharata lives because its characters still walk among us—**in us**.

You have met them in these pages.

Now carry them within:

- Let **Draupadi** give you a voice when you are silenced
- Let **Bhima** teach you loyalty and emotional honesty
- Let **Abhimanyu** remind you to take bold steps, but with guidance
- Let **Shakuni** warn you against cunning disguised as strategy
- Let **Krishna and Arjuna** guide you from conflict to contribution

This is not mythology.

This is **your dharmic design**.

Final Reflection – What You Must Remember

1. You are already enough. But you are not yet complete. Keep growing.
2. You cannot avoid every battle. But you can choose how to fight it.

3. Leadership is not about being perfect. It's about being present.
4. Wisdom doesn't shout. It whispers—when you're silent enough to listen.
5. Every day you have a choice: **React to the world, or respond to your dharma**.

Your Final Call to Action

> *"When doubt surrounds you, and action frightens you—stand still. Listen within. And choose dharma."*
>
> **– You are not here to survive.**
>
> **You are here to awaken.**

From today:

- Be your own Krishna. Guide yourself with truth and poise.
- Be your own Arjuna. Act with boldness and emotional integrity.
- And above all—lead with wisdom. Not because the world demands it.

But because your **soul remembers it**.

This is your **Kurukshetra Within**.

And you are ready.

APPENDICES

Appendix A1: The Mahabharata Leadership Archetype Quiz

Discover Which Archetype Guides Your Leadership Journey

"Leadership is not a fixed identity. It is a dynamic play of energy, values, and context."

– Inspired by the many faces of leadership in the Mahabharata

---

Purpose of the Quiz

This quiz is designed to help you:

- Reflect on your natural leadership tendencies
- Understand your responses to pressure, conflict, and responsibility
- Discover which Mahabharata archetype best mirrors your leadership style
- Gain insights on how to balance your strengths and blind spots

---

Instructions

- Answer each question honestly based on your typical behaviour at work or during high-pressure situations.

- Choose only **one option per question**.
- Tally the number of responses for each letter (A, B, C, D, E, F) at the end to find your archetype.
- Multiple top scores? That's okay — you might be a blend of archetypes, and that's a strength.

The Quiz (15 Questions)

1. **When faced with conflict in a team, you tend to:**
   A. Calmly guide the group toward a bigger picture
   B. Step up and lead with courage and clarity
   C. Speak up with passion, sometimes emotionally
   D. Dive into action without overthinking
   E. Trust your instincts and move even with half the information
   F. Observe quietly and use influence behind the scenes

---

2. **Your teammates would describe you as:**
   A. Wise and composed
   B. Brave and dependable
   C. Empathetic and vocal
   D. Fierce and loyal
   E. Energetic and daring
   F. Strategic and persuasive

---

3. **When under pressure, your first instinct is to:**
   A. Reflect and realign your values

B. Fight through it with focused execution
C. Express your emotions or seek justice
D. Take matters into your own hands
E. Trust your energy and move quickly
F. Use your intellect to control the situation subtly

---

4. What matters most to you in leadership?

A. Guiding others toward a purpose
B. Doing what is right, even if it's hard
C. Standing up for the voiceless
D. Protecting your team fiercely
E. Solving problems fearlessly
F. Influencing outcomes behind the scenes

---

5. Your leadership strength is:

A. Clarity of vision
B. Ethical courage
C. Emotional depth
D. Action-oriented loyalty
E. Boldness and intuition
F. Tact and long-term thinking

---

6. Your leadership blind spot is:

A. Being too detached or passive
B. Carrying the weight of the world
C. Letting emotion cloud logic

D. Acting without full consideration
E. Overconfidence in limited information
F. Manipulating without transparency

---

7. How do you handle office politics?

A. Rise above and focus on a higher purpose
B. Speak out and uphold fairness
C. Call it out emotionally
D. Confront it directly
E. Navigate it with enthusiasm, not strategy
F. Play the game to your advantage

---

8. What is your biggest internal challenge?

A. Detachment vs. involvement
B. Morality vs. duty
C. Expression vs. restraint
D. Anger vs. control
E. Overload vs. readiness
F. Integrity vs. manipulation

9.How do you recharge yourself?

A. Meditation, reflection, solitude
B. Serving or mentoring others
C. Speaking with a confidant
D. Physical activity, nature, or sport
E. Creative action or experimentation
F. Strategic planning or reading people

10. When leading a project, you are most likely to:

A. Serve as the invisible backbone
B. Define the big 'why' and drive purpose
C. Ensure fairness and representation
D. Push for speed and deliverables
E. Energize the group with enthusiasm
F. Secure outcomes through networks and influence

11. How do you respond to injustice?

A. Find a peaceful, principled resolution
B. Confront it directly and seek redress
C. Express outrage and rally others
D. Protect the victim at any cost
E. Dive in emotionally and impulsively
F. Use information and leverage to shift power

12. What type of leader inspires you most?

A. Visionary and detached
B. Warrior with purpose
C. Honest and empathetic
D. Loyal protector
E. Bold pioneer
F. Strategic thinker

13. How do you prefer to communicate during a crisis?

A. Ask questions, listen deeply
B. Give clear, directive action
C. Use emotion to connect
D. State facts and take control
E. Motivate with energy
F. Redirect conversations subtly

---

14. What's your biggest leadership fear?

A. Being unable to help others in time
B. Compromising on your values
C. Being misunderstood or unheard
D. Failing to protect your team
E. Being seen as naive
F. Being exposed or mistrusted

---

15. You define success as:

A. Uplifting others through guidance
B. Living with integrity, even under fire
C. Expressing truth and seeing justice done
D. Accomplishing goals with strength and loyalty
E. Growing through challenge and impact
F. Winning influence without being obvious

Results: Tally Your Answers

Count how many of each letter you selected:

- **Mostly A: Krishna** – The Wise Strategist
- **Mostly B: Arjuna** – The Conscious Warrior
- **Mostly C: Draupadi** – The Voice of Truth and Justice
- **Mostly D: Bhima** – The Protector and Force of Action
- **Mostly E: Abhimanyu** – The Bold Millennial Hero
- **Mostly F: Shakuni** – The Shadow Strategist (use with self-awareness)

What Your Archetype Means

Krishna (A)

You lead from behind the scenes, using clarity, calm, and deep wisdom. Your strength is influence without ego. Beware of detachment when action is needed.

Arjuna (B)

You are a purpose-led warrior with a strong moral compass. Your biggest growth comes from balancing confidence with compassion.

Draupadi (C)

You are emotionally intelligent, expressive, and a protector of justice. Your challenge is learning when to speak and when to conserve energy.

Bhima (D)

You are the team's shield—fiercely loyal, grounded, and dependable. Your task is channelling anger into meaningful action and learning softness.

Abhimanyu (E)

You are courageous, innovative, and eager to make an impact. You must seek mentorship and pause before diving headfirst into complex battles.

Shakuni (F)

You are intellectually sharp, observant, and highly strategic. If unchecked, you may resort to manipulation. Channel your insight into *transparent influence.*

Closing Note

No archetype is perfect — each carries light and shadow.

You are not **just one** of these. You are a dance of many, evolving through experience.

"In some moments, be Arjuna. In others, Krishna. But always be conscious of the war within—and the wisdom beyond."

APPENDIX A2: CONFLICT SCENARIOS AND RESPONSES

Epic vs. Corporate – Wisdom for the Modern Battleground

"Conflict is not the enemy. It is the invitation to choose between ego and evolution."

– Drawing parallels between Kurukshetra and the modern boardroom

---

How to Use This Appendix?

Each scenario below highlights:

- A **conflict situation** from today's workplace
- Its **Mahabharata equivalent**
- The typical **reactive response**
- The **epic-inspired dharmic response**

Use these reflections to deepen your awareness of your own choices—and to transform the way you lead and resolve tension.

⚔1. Power Struggle in Leadership

- **Corporate Scenario**: Two senior leaders compete for a promotion. One starts undermining the other through subtle politics.
- **Mahabharata Parallel**: Duryodhana vs. Yudhishthira — the fight for supremacy masked as entitlement.
- **Reactive Response**: Join the politics, defend reputation aggressively.
- **Dharmic Response**: Stay rooted in integrity (Yudhishthira). Let merit and conduct speak. Build alliances without stooping to sabotage. Seek a Krishna-like mentor to guide clarity.

⚔2. Not Being Recognized for Hard Work

- **Corporate Scenario**: You work tirelessly on a major project, but someone else takes the credit.
- **Mahabharata Parallel**: Karna's loyalty and effort under Duryodhana went unappreciated by many.
- **Reactive Response**: Rage, withdrawal, or quit abruptly.
- **Dharmic Response**: Like Karna, stay committed to excellence, but unlike Karna—**don't tie self-worth to external validation**. Learn to balance loyalty with self-respect.

⚔3. Handling Unethical Decisions

- **Corporate Scenario**: Leadership asks you to hide data or manipulate facts to please clients or investors.

- **Mahabharata Parallel**: Yudhishthira's dice game — silence in the face of dharma loss.
- **Reactive Response**: Obey silently, or quit in anger.
- **Dharmic Response**: Speak up respectfully (like Vidura), seek alternate solutions. Create a written ethical objection. Be clear: obedience ≠ integrity.

⚔4. Team Conflict Over Vision

- **Corporate Scenario**: Two departments clash over direction—tech vs. sales, strategy vs. execution.
- **Mahabharata Parallel**: Kauravas vs. Pandavas — different views of leadership and governance.
- **Reactive Response**: Label the other group "difficult" and disengage.
- **Dharmic Response**: Like Krishna, mediate with clarity. Focus on shared purpose over ego. Use structured dialogue to align teams.

⚔5. Emotional Burnout from Over-commitment

- **Corporate Scenario**: You're managing too much — stretched across deadlines, expectations, and emotional labour.
- **Mahabharata Parallel**: Arjuna on the eve of battle—paralyzed despite ability.
- **Reactive Response**: Breakdown, absenteeism, or detachment.

- **Dharmic Response**: Pause and reflect. Seek guidance (Gita moment). Reconnect with **purpose over performance**. Take a strategic retreat if needed.

⚔6. Being Undermined by a Peer

- **Corporate Scenario**: A colleague subtly discredits you in front of leadership while pretending to be supportive.
- **Mahabharata Parallel**: Shakuni's manipulation beneath diplomacy.
- **Reactive Response**: Call out publicly or retaliate quietly.
- **Dharmic Response**: Like Krishna, **see through intent** without immediate aggression. Build influence with transparency. Keep evidence, stay alert, and act with timing.

⚔7. Dealing with a Toxic Boss

- **Corporate Scenario**: A superior micromanages, manipulates, or humiliates consistently.
- **Mahabharata Parallel**: Dronacharya's dual role — nurturing talent but compromising dharma under pressure.
- **Reactive Response**: Passive compliance or explosive rebellion.
- **Dharmic Response**: Set **emotional and professional boundaries** (Bhima's silent resistance). Use feedback systems or seek internal allies. When the line is crossed repeatedly—exit with grace, not trauma.

⚔8. Managing a High-Risk Project with Unclear Ownership

- **Corporate Scenario**: You're assigned a critical project with limited clarity, mentorship, or support.
- **Mahabharata Parallel**: Abhimanyu entering the Chakravyuha — brave but underprepared.
- **Reactive Response**: Panic, over-promise, or break down mid-way.
- **Dharmic Response**: Ask for structure, mentors, and **build clarity before entry**. Know that **courage must be matched with systems.** Don't enter alone.

⚔9. Silenced for Speaking the Truth

- **Corporate Scenario**: You challenge an unfair policy or leader and face consequences.
- **Mahabharata Parallel**: Draupadi's insult in court — truth ignored due to power dynamics.
- **Reactive Response**: Leave silently or keep fighting in bitterness.
- **Dharmic Response**: Choose your moment. Speak like Draupadi — with poise and courage. If unheard, **document and escalate** wisely. Use platforms that protect your voice.

⚔10. Guilt After a Conflict is Won

- **Corporate Scenario**: You succeeded in your goal, but some relationships or values got compromised in the process.

- **Mahabharata Parallel**: Yudhishthira's post-war despair—victory without peace.
- **Reactive Response**: Suppress it or justify it.
- **Dharmic Response**: Acknowledge the cost. Seek emotional closure (as the Pandavas did through pilgrimage and counsel). Make amends where possible. Let guilt lead to growth, not paralysis.

💡 Closing Wisdom: Let Conflict Teach, Not Break You

Conflict is a test. Not of power, but of:

- Self-awareness
- Ethical clarity
- Emotional maturity
- Long-term thinking

"In every boardroom, Kurukshetra, choose Krishna's counsel over Duryodhana's certainty."

"In every challenge, ask: What would a dharmic leader do here?"

APPENDIX A3: GLOSSARY OF EPIC TERMS FOR MODERN MINDS

Translating Dharma for the Digital Age

"The words may be ancient, but their relevance is timeless."

— **Aligning epic vocabulary with everyday leadership**

Key Epic Concepts and Their Modern Reflections

---

1. Dharma (धर्म)

Traditional Meaning: Righteousness, duty, purpose, moral law

Modern Reflection: Your personal code of values. Ethical leadership. Doing the right thing—even when it's hard.

🧭 *Dharma is not a job role. It's your inner compass.*

---

2. Karma (कर्म)

Traditional Meaning: Action and its consequence

Modern Reflection: Cause and effect in behaviour. What you choose now shapes your tomorrow—emails, decisions, silence, and words included.

⚖ *Everything you do carries weight—visible or invisible.*

---

3. Kurukshetra (कुरुक्षेत्र)

Traditional Meaning: The battlefield where the Mahabharata war was fought

Modern Reflection: Your daily environment of challenge—your office, your mind, your relationships.

🎯 *The real Kurukshetra is not out there. It's within.*

---

4. Arjuna

Traditional Role: The warrior-prince, symbol of skill, confusion, and transformation

Modern Reflection: The modern professional seeking clarity in chaos. Talented but emotionally complex.

🧠 *Arjuna reminds us that even the best performers can break—and rebuild.*

---

5. Krishna

Traditional Role: Divine guide, charioteer, strategist

Modern Reflection: Your inner voice of wisdom. Your mentor, coach, or that moment of deep clarity.

🕊 *Be your own Krishna in moments of doubt.*

---

6. Yudhishthira

Traditional Role: Eldest Pandava, dharmic king

Modern Reflection: The ethical leader is often torn between idealism and leadership decisions.

⚖ *Being good doesn't guarantee comfort—but it grounds trust.*

---

7. Draupadi

Traditional Role: Empress, symbol of dignity, rage, and justice

Modern Reflection: The voice of emotional truth and power. Often ignored, yet central to change.

🔥 *Draupadi teaches us the cost of silence and the courage of speech.*

---

8. Bhima

Traditional Role: Strongest Pandava, emotional and loyal

Modern Reflection: The emotionally honest team player. Protective and action-oriented, but struggles with restraint.

Use Bhima's fire to protect, not to punish.

---

9. Abhimanyu

Traditional Role: Young warrior who entered a complex formation (Chakravyuha) without knowing how to exit

Modern Reflection: The ambitious, talented young professional with high risk and high potential.

Train before you enter complexity. Boldness must meet mentorship.

---

10. Shakuni

Traditional Role: The manipulative uncle, master of subtle sabotage

Modern Reflection: Symbol of office politics, hidden agendas, and long-term manipulation.

Know the Shakuni's around you—but don't become one.

---

11. Chakravyuha (चक्रव्यूह)

Traditional Meaning: A complex circular war formation

Modern Reflection: Any multi-layered system, bureaucracy, or high-stakes problem you enter without full context

Learn the system before you challenge it.

---

12. Gita (गीता)

Traditional Meaning: The Bhagavad Gita – spiritual dialogue between Krishna and Arjuna

Modern Reflection: A guidebook for ethical decision-making under pressure. Wisdom in motion.

Your daily reflections, therapy, or coaching session is your Gita moment.

---

13. Varna (वर्ण)

Traditional Meaning: Class or role in society (misinterpreted as caste)

Modern Reflection: Your personal strength profile—creator, strategist, implementer, healer, etc.

Know your natural leadership archetype—not everyone must be on stage.

---

14. Anartha (अनर्थ)

Traditional Meaning: Meaninglessness, loss, tragedy caused by ego or error

Modern Reflection: Self-sabotage. Avoidable chaos caused by unchecked pride or reactivity.

⊖ *The war within is often the source of outside breakdown.*

---

15. Samatvam (समत्वम्)

Traditional Meaning: Equanimity or balanced mind

Modern Reflection: Emotional regulation. Responding, not reacting. Staying centered.

Samatvam is your leadership superpower in chaos.

---

16. Tyaga (त्याग)

Traditional Meaning: Renunciation or sacrifice

Modern Reflection: Letting go of ego, outcome obsession, or control. Choosing purpose over possession.

ॐ *Tyaga is not about quitting. It's about releasing what holds you back.*

---

17. Atma (आत्मा)

Traditional Meaning: The true self, soul, or inner essence

Modern Reflection: Your most authentic self beyond role, title, and performance metrics

You are not your LinkedIn bio. You are your intention.

Final Thought

"When ancient wisdom meets modern reflection, leadership transforms from strategy into service."

Let this glossary remind you that you're not just navigating tasks—you're walking a path of transformation, guided by voices thousands of years old and deeply present in your daily decisions.

APPENDIX A4: DAILY DHARMA FRAMEWORK FOR PROFESSIONALS

Live. Lead. Decide. The Mahabharata Way.

"Your work is not separate from your values.

It is where your values are tested—and forged."

🎯 Purpose of the Framework

The **Daily Dharma Framework** is designed to:

- Help professionals align **values with action**
- Cultivate mindful leadership habits
- Build emotional resilience under pressure
- Integrate the teachings of Krishna, Arjuna, Bhima, Draupadi, and Abhimanyu into your work life

It's not about doing more.

It's about **doing what matters—consciously**.

🧭 The 5-Pillar Dharma Framework

Each day, reflect on and act through these five pillars. Together, they form the acronym: **D.H.A.R.M.A.**

D – Define Your Inner Intention (Krishna's Clarity)

Start your day with one simple question:

🧘 *"What kind of person and professional do I want to be today?"*

Daily Practice:

- Write down 1–2 core values for the day (e.g., honesty, patience, creativity)
- Take 2 minutes to visualize one situation where you might need to **pause before you act**

Why it works:

It centers you before the world pulls you in.

H – Honour Your Energy (Bhima's Awareness)

Track your **energy, not just your time.**

Daily Practice:

- Midday: Do a quick **Energy Audit**

Ask: Am I reacting or responding?

- If drained, take a pause — walk, hydrate, breathe.

Tip: Energy mismanagement leads to emotional mismanagement.

A – Act from Dharma, Not Drama (Draupadi's Courage)

Every day offers you triggers. Choose how you respond.

Daily Practice:

- Before a challenging conversation or decision, ask:

"Is this coming from ego or from purpose?"

- Use the **Pause → Breathe → Respond** model.

Why it matters:

When emotions guide action, consequences often last longer than the moment.

R – Reflect Without Judgment (Arjuna's Introspection)

You don't have to be perfect. But you must be aware.

Daily Practice:

- End your day with 3 journaling prompts:

1. What did I do well today?
2. Where did I stray from my values?
3. What is one thing I'll shift tomorrow?

Even 5 minutes of reflection builds self-leadership.

M – Maintain Meaningful Boundaries (Abhimanyu's Lesson)

Don't enter every fight or problem unprepared.

Daily Practice:

- Say **NO** to one non-essential task or meeting
- Protect your deep work and emotional space like sacred ground
- Ask: *"Do I have enough clarity/support to take this on?"*

Remember: Not every battle is yours to fight.

A – Align Your Actions with a Bigger Purpose (Yudhishthira's Legacy)

Purpose is not a long-term vision. It's a **daily orientation.**

Daily Practice:

- Before closing your day, ask:

"Did today reflect the kind of impact I want to leave behind?"

- Each week, reconnect with your "why":

What kind of leader, friend, and human am I becoming?

Outcome: Progress feels better than perfection.

🧘 Optional: Daily Dharma Check-In Card

You can print or write this on a sticky note for your desk:

🪷 Daily Dharma Card

Today's Intention: ______________________

One Energy Reset Plan: ______________________

My Dharma Decision Cue:

"I will pause when I feel triggered."

Boundary to Honour: __________________________

Evening Reflection:

- Win: ___________________________
- Lesson: _________________________
- Shift: ___________________________

💬 Closing Wisdom

"Don't just manage time. Manage your soul's alignment."

"In a world of speed, Dharma is your anchor."

This framework isn't rigid—it's **alive**. Use it daily, weekly, or even in moments of chaos to return to your center.

The battlefield won't disappear.

But your ability to lead through it—with clarity, calm, and courage—will grow.